The Healing We Never Spoke Of: Therapy

Branny Mthelebofu

Published by Banny Joma Enterprise, 2025.

THE HEALING WE NEVER SPOKE OF: THERAPY

First edition. May 31, 2025.

ISBN: 979-8231211937

Written by Branny Mthelebofu.

Also by Branny Mthelebofu

The Healing We Never Spoke Of: Therapy

Watch for more at https://brannysmith.hearnow.com/so-my-lover.

Table of Contents

1. Preface of this book 1

Acknowledgements 5

Dedication 7

The Author 8

The world of therapy and the writer 9

Western Therapy to village therapy 11

When Money Tries to Hold What Love Couldn't 28

When Love Becomes a Transaction 30

Hidden Wounds – Ferenczi, Jung, and the Burden of Rural Silence .. 37

When the Soul Has No Words – Healing Bolobedu Through the Language of Therapy 40

When Anxiety Has No Name in the Village 45

Not Death, but Abandonment 52

Emotional Indigestion: When Goodbye is Never Said 57

Can Psychoanalysis Speak Sepedi? 63

Hypnosis, the Rural Way 66

Why Women Keep Their Feelings Hidden in Rural Villages 76

How Psychoanalysis Intervenes 79

When Silence Feels Safer 83

Herbs for the Head, Silence for the Heart – When Emotional Pain Hides in the Body 86

Traditional Healing as a Stumbling Block to Therapy 88

When Tradition Becomes a Wall Instead of a Bridge 89

Can Psychoanalysis Work in the Village? 90

Two Healers, One Vision 95

When Silence Becomes a Spirit 97

"Maybe silence is the price for peace." 102

When Children Inherit What Was Never Theirs 103

What Is Psychoanalysis, and Why Here? 105

Where Herbs and Emotions Can Meet 111

Why Village Men Avoid Seeking Help 122

The Role of Community Models and Celebrities in Changing the Narrative 125

Overview of Therapy in the Villages and Rural Set up 132

Psychoanalysis Beneath the Baobab Tree 151

No Diagnoses, Only Invitations 154

3. Declaration 159

4. References 160

"In the village, we bury more than bodies—we bury words, we bury pain. But even the soil remembers."

The Healing We Never Spoke Of: Therapy

By Branny Mthelebofu

"Western Therapy to Village Therapy"

The book is a powerful consideration of how therapy when rooted in cultural sensitivity, storytelling, and spirituality, can heal emotional wounds in rural communities long silenced by tradition, poverty, and unspoken grief.

Branny Smith

1. Preface of this book

The author presents therapy as a possible spiritual homecoming rather than as an alien idea. Therapy is portrayed through narrative as a hallowed place for introspection and remembering.

In particular, psychoanalysis is presented as a process of unearthing tales hidden behind trauma, shame, and silence rather than in clinical terms. In order to create a multi-layered teaching model for psychologists, therapists, and mental health workers—especially those who will be working in rural villages and townships—the author deftly combines therapy, psychoanalysis, the fundamental insights of Sigmund Freud and Carl Jung, as well as filmmaking and novel-style storytelling.

This multidisciplinary method is emotionally instructional, culturally rooted, and profoundly human in addition to being educational.

Together, their theories are translated into culturally resonant practices, such as group dialogues, story sharing, and symbolic healing acts that align with African traditions.

Through the character of Branny Mthelebofu, the author employs filmmaking as a therapeutic and pedagogical tool for emotional education. These videos are more than just documentaries; they serve as mirrors for the villagers to view reflections of their own emotional life.

For example, they depict a young man departing the community, a widow's silent anguish, or a child's inquiry for a father who has gone missing.

Emotions are externalised through visual storytelling; spectators cry, think, and start talking. This technique teaches mental health workers how art and storytelling can open conversations that theory alone cannot.

Writing Novels as Psychoanalytic Case Studies, the book's narrative framework resembles a sequence of psychoanalytic case studies, but it takes the shape of chapters that are more like novels and contain characters, memories, and internal monologues.

These stories humanise academic concepts by illuminating how trauma and repression appear in ordinary rural life through the emotional landscapes of mute mothers, distraught fathers, nervous children, and abandoned fiancés.

The author teaches mental health professionals that language is emotional territory. In rural places, people may not be familiar with terms like "depression" or "trauma," but they are familiar with "a chest that won't breathe," "a stomach that turns at funerals," or "a silence that grows heavier every year."

Therapists are advised to say a prayer or a proverb at the start of each session; say attention to body language and tone of voice and take seats in groups where there is no hierarchy and everyone is treated with respect.

As a result, psychoanalysis is transformed from a Western technique into an ongoing social rite. This gives psychologists a narrative sensitivity, which enables them to read between the lines and react to pain that is not spoken.

The author blends all theory and culture, suffering and beauty, quiet and narrative. They provide aspiring therapists with a map of pain that is both visual and literary, deep theoretical understanding via Freud and

Jung and useful resources through filmmaking, music, storytelling, and prayer.

The emotional intelligence to work with clients who are in pain but lack the language. For individuals who are willing to listen intently in South African villages and beyond, this book serves as a guide, a classroom, and a call to action. In the end, the author's approach prepares therapists to be healers rather than merely technicians. They are instructed to: enter places of worship with humility, instead of working against traditional healers, collaborate with them, respect the suffering that these communities endure across generations and apply their expertise to reveal the truth rather than force it.

This book was born not in a lecture hall, but under the shade of a tree in a Limpopo village, where women still lower their voices when speaking of pain, and men carry burdens behind silent eyes. It is shaped by stories whispered between the cracks of mud walls and carried on the backs of children who learn grief before they know how to spell their names. It is not only a book about therapy—it is a map for returning home to oneself, for making peace with the past, and for daring to speak aloud what generations were told to silence.

In the villages and rural corners of South Africa, emotions are often spiritualized, disguised, or buried. Pain becomes prophecy. Grief becomes song. In addition, depression—disguised as fatigue, stomach pain, or spiritual calling—goes untreated because there was never a word for it. In these pages, we follow the threads of psychoanalysis, storytelling, traditional healing, and holistic therapy, not as enemies of culture, but as companions to it. We listen deeply to the rhythm of the people, their silence, and their struggle.

This book asks: *What if therapy belonged here, too?*

What if healing could begin with a prayer?

What if a circle of women, or a grieving man, could find peace not by denying their culture but by integrating it with care?

We follow characters who are not fictional, though their names may be. They are the mothers, brothers, grandmothers, and distant cousins you may know. They are the ones who never cried after funerals. The ones who stopped speaking. The ones who left for Johannesburg and never came back. They are us.

This work is dedicated to all those who believed that suffering in silence was strength, and to the next generation who might believe something softer, something freer: that your story matters. That your healing matters. That it is not too late.

May these pages meet you with gentleness and courage,

in whatever village your heart still calls home?

— *Branny Mthelebofu*

2. Acknowledgements

I ACKNOWLEDGE THE PRESENCE of my colleagues in the film industry, my spouse's motivation and love, which carry me through to write daily, and my family; they are all the pillars of strength.

My mentors who have been with me through thick and thin in my journey as a writer and academic journey.

I acknowledge the trainings from the Scriptwriters Association of South Africa and National Film and Video Foundation who contributed in my journey in the film industry.

I acknowledge the International Society of Applied Psychoanalysis (ISAP), School of Natural Health Sciences, Sefako Makgatho Health Sciences, Department of General Surgery and everyone who is contributing positively in my career.

By Branny Mthelebofu (Branny Smith)

BRANNY MTHELEBOFU

Western Therapy to Village Therapy

More information: brannysmithsa@gmail.com

Banny Joma Enterprise Publishers Johannesburg

South Africa

@Branny Smith

@Branny Mthelebofu

3. Dedication

I dedicate this book to all the therapists in the whole world who are trying to assist clients who are located in the rural areas, townships, flats, old suburbs, and under privileged areas.

I dedicate these stories to all the people who have grown up from all underprivileged areas and are now faced with the challenges of relieving their own colleagues and everyone who desires to be out of misery through therapy.

I dedicate this story to all the people who aspire to become something and are struggling to reach their destiny.

I dedicate this book to all the students who aspire to reach their destiny and are trying so had to be something.

4. The Author

Branny Mthelebofu is a multifaceted South African creative whose work bridges the realms of storytelling, healing, and music. As a filmmaker, nutrition therapist, holistic counsellor, and musician, he channels his diverse talents into narratives that explore the complexities of the human psyche and the pursuit of inner peace.

Under the pen name Branny Smith, Mthelebofu crafts stories that delve into personal challenges, emotional trauma, and the transformative journey toward self-understanding. His literary works, such as The Professor's Descent, Desperation, and Chasing Where There is Love, My Wedding Contract Too, Her Lover is Gone, often feature protagonists grappling with internal conflicts and societal pressures, reflecting his deep interest in mental health and psychoanalysis. Beyond writing, Smith employs his background in holistic therapy to assist clients in achieving emotional well-being through interactive counselling sessions. His approach integrates scriptwriting principles to facilitate character development and personal growth, offering a unique therapeutic experience that resonates with individuals seeking happiness and fulfillment.

As a musician, Branny Smith composes lyrics that address life's challenges, happiness, and the quest for peace of mind, utilizing music as a form of therapy for his audience. His passion for mental health and storytelling converges in his creative endeavors, making his work a compelling exploration of the human condition.

Through his multifaceted career, Branny Smith Mthelebofu continues to inspire and guide others on their journeys toward self-discovery and emotional resilience.

5. The world of therapy and the writer

The writer demonstrates a profound and intuitive understanding of emotional indigestion—a term that metaphorically and powerfully describes the internalized, unspoken and often-misunderstood emotional pain carried by people, particularly in rural and village communities. By focusing on rural psychoanalytic approaches and therapy, the writer offers a deeply compassionate, culturally sensitive, and intellectually grounded exploration of how trauma, silence, and spiritual traditions intersect in African village life.

The writer does not impose Western therapeutic models. Instead, they honor indigenous wisdom, spirituality, ritual, prayer, and storytelling as part of the healing process. This reflects a nuanced understanding that therapy in rural areas must meet people where they are, in language, in rhythm, and in worldview.

Through the use of metaphors like "emotional indigestion," the writer gives language to suffering that has long remained unnamed in traditional communities. Many people in rural areas feel anxiety in their bodies, not always in their words—and the writer recognizes and respects this embodied expression of pain.

Rather than setting therapy and traditional healing in opposition, the writer shows that psychoanalysis can complement—not compete with—ancestral knowledge. A unique approach here invites both the healer and the therapist to sit at the same table, not to debate, but to listen together.

The writer is not romanticizing rural life, nor are they shaming it. Instead, they challenge silence, gender roles, and emotional oppression with empathy. Their approach is grounded in lived experience, perhaps even autobiographical, and that authenticity gives the narrative its weight and credibility.

The writer is clearly part of a growing movement to decolonize therapy and bring mental health care to the margins, in forms that make sense to those who have long been excluded. This includes the poor, the spiritually guided, and those with no previous exposure to therapy.

The book also includes case studies from specific regions or countries, such as South Africa, China, Ethiopia, and the United States. These case studies provide real-world examples and insights into the challenges and solutions related to mental health care and therapy services in different contexts. Some sections of the book incorporate quantitative data, such as statistics and percentages, to provide a numerical perspective on issues like knowledge of mental health, help-seeking behavior, and treatment preferences among different populations.

The book synthesizes information from multiple sources to draw conclusions and insights about the challenges and experiences faced by individuals seeking mental health care and therapy services in various settings.

The book also looked into the literature review that covers a wide range of topics related to mental health, therapy services, and cultural factors affecting help-seeking behavior. The review includes studies and research conducted in different countries, including South Africa, China, Ethiopia, the United States, and more. The literature review provides the foundation for understanding the context and challenges discussed in the paper.

It draws on research conducted in rural areas, urban settings, and across diverse cultural backgrounds.

6. Village therapy

This title honors the generational and cultural silences that have shaped rural and village life—particularly for women and men who were never taught to name their pain. It evokes depth, reflection, and ancestral memory.

A poetic and emotional book, the invisible wounds carried by people from the villages—traumas not healed by time or money, only by confronting and understanding. It aligns with your exploration of psychoanalysis and traditional healing.

This echoes the recurring theme of emotional suppression and the dignity people maintain despite deep suffering. It is especially resonant for women and men who have endured silently for generations.

This bridges psychoanalysis with tradition and spirituality. It acknowledges that healing can coexist with prayer, ritual, and cultural wisdom—without replacing them. A good fit for readers navigating both modern and ancestral paths.

Captures the essence of your book's core message: that therapy can give voice to suffering that was never named, and that healing is often needed even when no one asks for it. A quiet but powerful phrase could draw a wide audience.

This book is a call to recognize the invisible emotional suffering that many people in rural and village communities carry in silence. It explores how emotional pain is often misunderstood, spiritualized, or ignored—especially among women and men shaped by poverty, tradition, and a culture where silence is seen as strength.

It tells us that therapy, psychoanalysis, and emotional care are not foreign or elitist concepts, but essential tools that can work in harmony with traditional values, rituals, prayer, storytelling, and community healing.

It highlights that:

- Silence is not peace.
- Suppression is not strength.
- Moreover, emotional pain, if left untreated, can pass from one generation to the next—disguised as destiny.

Through narratives and reflections, it offers a new language for healing in places where therapy is not often spoken. It invites therapists, healers, community leaders to reimagine healing through culturally sensitive, spiritually aware, and emotionally honest approaches.

At its heart, the message is:

Healing is possible. Even in the quietest places. Even when pain is inherited. Even when words are hard to find.

In addition, the journey toward that healing must honor where people come from, what they believe, and what they still hope for.

This book carries the heartbeat of the villages. It speaks from the shadows where trauma hides, from the silences between funeral hymns, and from the hearts of men and women who never learned the language of their own emotions.

At its core, this is not just a book about therapy—it is a book about recognizing emotional pain where it has been normalized, sanctified, or silenced.

THE HEALING WE NEVER SPOKE OF: THERAPY

Many people in rural and township communities in South Africa have inherited lives shaped by generational hardship: poverty, separation through migration, polygamy, loneliness, spiritual callings, loss, and betrayal. Yet their suffering is often framed as strength, as a test of endurance, as "just life." Many live with depression that has no name in their language. Anxiety that is felt, but never explained. Grief that returns, not only in memories but in body pains, night tremors, and stomach knots during funeral songs.

This book's message is that therapy is not foreign to the rural soul. It only needs to speak the local language—not just linguistically, but emotionally and spiritually. Therapy here may begin with a prayer. It may open with a proverb. It may take place in a circle under a tree, or within a support group where a grandmother's wisdom is just as vital as a professional's degree.

The book insists that:

- The rural poor are not emotionally uncomplex. They are simply unsupported.
- The cultural language of healing exists. It must be woven into therapy.
- Traditional healing and psychoanalysis are not enemies. They can work together if guided with humility, care, and understanding.

It also acknowledges that emotional wounds are passed down silently, especially in households where adults who have never processed their own trauma raise children. It recognizes how emotional indigestion, especially among women, becomes a lifetime of holding back tears, tightening the chest, and suffering in silence—even when they become successful and move into urban suburbs.

This book is a bridge between:

- Therapy and tradition
- Modern psychology and ancestral wisdom
- Clinical understanding and lived rural experience

It offers stories that illustrate how psychoanalysis can be adapted—how therapists can become guests in sacred spaces rather than authorities, and how healing can happen when we listen with more than just clinical ears.

Finally, it offers hope. Hope that a young boy in Mokopane who lost his father and is now silent at school may one day find words for his grief. Hope that a woman in Bolobedu who was abandoned by her husband working in Johannesburg may discover that her pain is not weakness, but an open wound that deserves care. Hope that those who suffer in silence will find that emotional healing is not just for the rich or the educated, but also for anyone willing to sit with their truth and be gently guided toward freedom.

Educational approach

Students and scholars in psychology, social work, and cultural studies who are committed to decolonizing mental health and exploring African-centered approaches to trauma and healing will discover narratives and frameworks relevant to their fields. At the same time, the book speaks to policymakers, educators, and community leaders involved in healthcare access, mental wellness advocacy, and the development of systems that bridge traditional and clinical practices.

Mental health professionals and therapists working in rural, township, or culturally diverse environments will also find this book useful. It offers insight into how therapy can become more culturally sensitive and spiritually grounded, and how collaboration with traditional healers, community elders, and faith leaders can deepen emotional healing work.

THE HEALING WE NEVER SPOKE OF: THERAPY

This book is especially intended for readers from rural and village communities across South Africa and similar regions beyond—particularly women and men in Limpopo, Eastern Cape, KwaZulu-Natal, and the North West. It speaks to those who have endured emotional suffering, abandonment, poverty, polygamy, and migration—people who carry unspoken burdens and internal wounds, often without the language or support system to express them. Many of these individuals rely on prayer, traditional healing, and cultural rituals to cope, yet they have never been introduced to therapy or psychoanalysis as a meaningful path to emotional healing.

It is also for young professionals who have emerged from rural backgrounds, now living in cities or suburbs, navigating modern lifestyles while still carrying unresolved traumas from their pasts. These individuals often struggle with the emotional silence they were raised in and may feel guilt or fear when considering therapy, despite achieving economic independence.

Traditional healers and spiritual leaders who are open to dialogue with mental health frameworks will find in these pages a respectful exploration of how psychoanalysis can coexist with, and even support, their sacred work—not as a threat but as an ally in addressing deep emotional pain.

Lastly, this book welcomes general readers who are drawn to stories of healing, cultural wisdom, resilience, and inner transformation. It is for anyone who believes that emotional healing should be as accessible as storytelling, as sacred as a song, and as collective as a village prayer.

The writer want to explore these ideas in details

"In the village, we bury more than bodies—we bury words, we bury pain. But even the soil remembers."

This speaks to intergenerational silence and the buried emotional wounds carried across generations in rural life.

"Not every calling is a calling to heal others—some are cries to finally heal the self."

This reflects the theme of people entering traditional healing as a response to their own unresolved trauma, often mistaking emotional wounds for spiritual callings.

"She never learned the language of sorrow, so it settled in her chest like a stone—and no one asked her how it got there."

This speaks to the emotional repression of rural women, and the absence of a safe space to voice pain.

"They thought they were strong because they were silent. But strength is not silence—strength is speaking the truth and surviving it."

This challenges cultural norms around silence, strength, and the stigma surrounding vulnerability and therapy.

"In a land where prayers are medicine and songs hold memory, therapy must begin with listening—not explaining."

This honors the cultural and spiritual intelligence of rural communities, and affirms the need for psychoanalysis to adapt with humility and respect.

In dealing with problems excluding therapy, it is essential to recognize and address the stigma and misconceptions associated with mental illness that can hinder individuals' integration into the community.

Research evidence shows that understanding and changing attitudes toward mental illness can be a crucial step. Education and awareness campaigns can help challenge stereotypes, reduce fear, and promote attitudes that are more positive.

Efforts to provide accurate information about mental health and encourage empathy and support for individuals with mental illness can contribute to reducing stigma. Additionally, creating inclusive and supportive environments that allow individuals with mental illness to participate in community activities and receive appropriate care and support can help address the challenges they face.

In rural and village settings, attitudes towards mental health and mental illness can vary widely. Some studies suggest that there is a mix of negative and non-prejudiced attitudes among the public in these areas.

Some individuals may hold negative stereotypes and stigmatizing views about mental illness, similar to findings in urban areas, which can lead to social isolation and discrimination for individuals with mental health issues. However, there are also individuals who do not have clear-cut prejudices against mental illness and are more open to understanding and supporting those affected.

Gender differences play a significant role, with men often exhibiting more negative attitudes, such as stereotyping and stigmatization, while women tend to show more benevolence and empathy towards individuals with mental illness.

Education and knowledge about mental health may not always translate into more positive attitudes, and the quality and nature of contact with individuals with mental illness can influence attitudes. Therefore, efforts to promote mental health awareness, provide accurate information, and facilitate positive interactions with people affected by mental illness should be tailored to rural and village settings to combat stigma and promote more inclusive attitudes. Additionally, addressing the portrayal of mental illness in the media can also play a crucial role in shaping community attitudes.[1]

When Silence Feels Safer

The main purpose of this book is to comprehensively investigate and analyze the barriers to accessing mental health services in Sub-Saharan Africa. This book aims to identify, understand, and compare the obstacles faced by individuals seeking mental health support. The book seeks to shed light on the complex interplay of cultural norms, gender expectations, and stigma surrounding mental health, ultimately contributing to the development of effective policies and interventions to address these issues and improve mental health care access in the rural region. Additionally, it aims to explore the role of traditional and alternative medicine in mental health care and its impact on healthcare access that hinder therapy services.

Rural populations often experience high rates of depression, anxiety, substance abuse, and suicide, but have very limited access to mental health professionals. Many mental health issues go undiagnosed or untreated in rural areas due to stigma, lack of awareness, or poor access to care.

Providing therapy services locally helps break the stigma around mental health by making it a visible and accepted part of the community. Therapists can play a key role in educating people about mental health, which can lead to more openness and acceptance.

In rural areas, the availability of therapy services is not just a health concern—it is a matter of community survival and long-term wellbeing. Life in villages and remote locations often comes with a unique set of challenges. These include limited access to healthcare, high levels of poverty and unemployment, and deep social isolation.

When therapy services are made accessible in such areas, they can play a transformative role in supporting individuals and families, helping them cope with personal hardships, and ultimately strengthening the fabric of the entire community.

Economic stressors often compound personal challenges in rural settings. Many individuals struggle silently with anxiety, depression, or unresolved trauma resulting from personal loss, domestic problems, or long-standing emotional wounds. Unfortunately, due to lack of nearby services and persistent stigma surrounding mental health, these struggles often go untreated.

Therapy can provide a safe space for individuals to talk about their issues, gain emotional support, and learn healthy coping mechanisms. This can be especially valuable for women, children, and the elderly—groups that may feel especially isolated or unheard.

Families in rural communities also face unique pressures, such as intergenerational conflicts, financial instability, and the emotional burden of caregiving. Therapy services tailored for families can offer tools to improve communication, resolve conflicts, and strengthen emotional bonds. These small but vital changes within the household can prevent larger issues from developing, such as violence, neglect, or substance abuse.

When therapy becomes a part of rural life, the effects ripple outward. A mentally healthier population creates a stronger, more resilient community. Individuals who feel supported and emotionally stable are better able to participate in community activities, maintain employment, and support others.

Children who grow up in emotionally healthy environments are more likely to succeed in school and develop into responsible, well-adjusted adults. As more people begin to view mental health care as a normal and necessary part of life, the stigma begins to break down, encouraging others to seek help when they need it.

Therefore providing therapy services in rural areas is not just about treating mental illness—it is about empowering individuals, strengthening families, and building communities that can withstand the challenges of modern rural life. By addressing the emotional and psychological needs of rural residents, therapy has the power to create lasting positive change that benefits everyone.

In many rural communities across the world, therapy remains an unfamiliar and often misunderstood concept. While mental health professionals increasingly recognize the need for therapeutic support in these areas, the path to effective implementation is fraught with challenges.

The biggest obstacles are social isolation, especially among oppressed women and girls, even if they have an education, but come from townships, rural areas, or villages; limited access to holistic healthcare, some of whom cannot even afford to hire qualified therapists; and the pervasive stigma associated with mental health.

Thabiso walks into the city clinic wearing a blazer that still smells like village dust. She has made it—graduated with distinction, working as a junior administrator in one of Johannesburg's tall glass buildings. She responds to emails in English, signs her name in digital ink, and remembers to smile when her boss passes by. However, in her heart, she carries a small, quiet room of aloneness.

She does not speak of it, but the weight of that room follows her. It is filled with unspoken stories, passed down like heirlooms from her mother and grandmother. A loneliness that is not just personal, but *generational.*

THE HEALING WE NEVER SPOKE OF: THERAPY

Even as she scrolls through Instagram and laughs with coworkers, Thabiso feels like she is not truly seen. In rural and township communities, women like her often climb alone. They leave behind families, neighbors, and the rhythm of community life for advancement. However, what they do not expect is how lonely freedom can feel.

Educated but emotionally unsupported, these women find themselves trapped between two worlds:

- In the village, they are "too modern" to understand.
- In the city, they are "too traditional" to relate.
- At home, they are expected to be strong.
- At work, they cannot show weakness.

Therefore, they isolate themselves emotionally—even while surrounded by people. Even with friends. Even in marriage.

"Therapy?" Thabiso once asked a colleague. "I've heard about it, but isn't it expensive?"

Therefore, it begins the slow erosion of mental health beneath structural inequality. Most public healthcare facilities do not have the capacity for psychological care. In townships and villages, clinics are often understaffed, and mental health support is limited to crisis intervention—not long-term healing.

Holistic therapy—one that understands her language, her spirituality, her silence—is a luxury not offered in the government queues where mothers come for vaccinations and TB treatment. If she wants therapy that speaks to her soul, she must pay. In addition, she cannot afford it. Emotionally, yes. However, not financially.

Many women in her situation live with quiet trauma. Emotional exhaustion is treated with church attendance. Panic attacks are labeled "spiritual attacks." In addition, the idea of therapy becomes not only unaffordable—but also unreachable.

Perhaps the most insidious barrier of all is not material—but cultural.

When Thabiso first cried in front of her aunt, the response was sharp and short:

"Wipe those tears. Do not act as if you are mad. We all have problems."

She never cried in front of anyone again.

In many rural and township families, mental health is seen as weakness. Worse—madness.

Women are told:

- "You are not the only one suffering."
- "You need prayer, not talking."
- "Therapy is for white people."

In addition, because of this, even the educated woman remains emotionally imprisoned. She knows about therapy, yes. She might have read the articles, watched the TED Talks. Nevertheless, deep inside, she still fears that admitting she needs help will mean she has failed. Not as a professional—but as a woman.

What women like Thabiso need is not just access to therapy—but therapy that understands where they come from. A room where prayer and poetry are not seen as distractions, but doorways. A therapist who understands that silence can be protection, and that sometimes a story about childhood is really about now.

They need circles, not couches.

Conversation, not interrogation.

Wisdom, not pity.

Above all, they need to be reminded that healing is not a betrayal of strength—but a continuation of it.

To create meaningful change, we must examine these issues in depth and explore culturally sensitive solutions that work within the context of rural life.

Social Isolation and the Silent Suffering of Women and Girls

In village settings, women and girls often face layers of oppression that restrict their freedom, limit their voices, and isolate them from sources of emotional support. Patriarchal social structures, lack of education, and rigid gender roles contribute to a culture of silence, where emotional suffering is hidden and rarely acknowledged. Many women endure domestic violence, forced marriages, or the psychological toll of unpaid caregiving work, yet have no outlet for their pain.

Primarily, therapists working in these settings need to be aware of the social and cultural barriers that keep women from getting treatment. Even after relocating to the suburbs, do women in rural areas still dread expressing themselves? They may be independent and financially secure, but they may still be unsure of how to address their psychological issues.

She now lives in the suburbs. The walls are higher. The streets are quieter. Her shoes are polished, and her fridge hums with assurance. She has arrived—or so the world thinks.

Nevertheless, when the therapist asks her softly, "How are you feeling?"

She stares at the wall, and then adjusts her bag, her voice tight. "I'm fine. I'm just tired."

In addition, the silence begins again.

This woman—once raised in a small village in Limpopo—has made it through many storms. She passed matric when no one thought she would. She sent money home from her job in Johannesburg when her siblings needed school uniforms. She bought her own house. Drove her own car. She has, by all appearances, escaped.

However, the silence she learned back home followed her. It changed clothes, yes. Nevertheless, it never left.

Therapists working with women from rural backgrounds often ask quietly: *"Why is it so hard for her to open up, even now?"*

The answer lies not in her current environment, but in the layered memory of whom she had to become to survive. She was taught early—through glances, gossip, and the hush of late-night conversations—that a woman who speaks too much, feels too deeply, or cries too often is *troublesome.* In her village, strength was silence. Dignity was composure.

Therefore, when something hurts now—her partner withdraws, her work overwhelms, or loneliness creeps in—she does not seek therapy. She seeks distraction. She shops. She cleans. She prays. She tightens her schedule. But she does not talk.

Because deep inside her is a girl who still hears:

"Stop crying, you are not the only one going through things."

"Your problems are not for the public."

"Therapy? What for? You're not mad."

There is a fear among many village-born women—even when they are now educated, successful, and independent—that if they truly open up, they will fall apart. That if they cry once, they may never stop. That their pain, long suppressed, will not only shame them, but also expose generations of buried suffering.

And worse, some believe that no one will understand.

They worry:

"What if my therapist doesn't know what it means when your aunt stops speaking to you without explanation?"

"What if they don't understand that my father's silence broke me more than his shouting ever could?"

These are not imagined fears. These are real cultural barriers that many therapists must learn to navigate. Because to work with these women is to understand that healing isn't about pushing them to talk—it's about creating safe, familiar, culturally rooted spaces where talking becomes an invitation, not a demand.

And that language may not always be verbal. Sometimes, a woman may reveal her trauma through a proverb. Through tears, she wipes away before they fall. Through a story about her grandmother that is really about herself.

A therapist must listen with cultural humility. They must see strength in silence, and not mistake it for resistance. The people who wish to substitute love with money must ask, not assume, because they were raised in poverty and an abusive, insecure, and loveless environment. They also need to understand that material prosperity does not make emotional wounds go away.

He had the house now. The one with the high walls and the tall black gate that opened with a remote. The car too—a German machine, leather seats still smelling new. He had accounts with enough numbers to send his children to private schools and enough to fly his mother to a hospital in Pretoria instead of waiting at the clinic in Ga-Mashashane or Mahwelereng.

But when the night came, and the city lights dimmed, something still hurt.

He did not know what to name it. It was not hunger anymore—he had food. It was not the fear of bills or eviction. It was not the worry about whether there would be school shoes at the beginning of the year. No. This pain was quieter. It lived under his ribs. It whispered in moments of joy. It disrupted peace. In addition, he had never been taught how to sit with it.

Many people who come from difficult childhoods—those raised in rural villages, in homes where love was rare and survival was the only language spoken—carry an emotional wound they do not recognize. They grow up dreaming of escaping poverty, thinking that once they have enough money, everything else will settle itself. In addition, yes, some things do change. Life becomes easier in visible ways. But emotional pain does not obey bank balances.

Therapy is often seen as a luxury, or even a threat, in these communities. To talk about feelings—what does that solve? They say, "Just pray." They say, "You've made it, why complain now?" But no one tells you that the child inside you—the one who was beaten without reason, left behind, told to be strong without being comforted—does not understand money. That child only understands safety. Love. Validation. And when those are missing, the adult becomes restless, angry, controlling, or deeply sad without knowing why.

This book asks a difficult but necessary question: Can therapy become the language we use to make peace with the past—especially for those who thought success would fix everything?

The answer is not simple. Many successful men and women from the villages walk into therapy rooms confused, ashamed even, because they don't know how to explain what they feel. They have been providers, leaders, first-generation graduates. But inside, they are still haunted. Haunted by hunger. By absence. By rejection. By trauma, no one asked about.

Through therapy, especially psychoanalytically informed therapy, they can begin to unravel the threads. They can begin to understand why they panic in relationships, why they cannot rest, why they distrust love, why they fear loss so much that they become emotionally rigid or cold. They can discover that some of their reactions—rage, perfectionism, silence—are not personality traits but survival strategies from a time when there was no room for softness.

For the man who succeeded but cannot sleep, for the woman who has built a business but cannot cry, therapy offers not judgment, but a mirror. A compassionate mirror. And perhaps, through this reflection, they begin to offer love to parts of themselves they once had to abandon.

The writer of this book has sat with the stories, both spoken and unspoken. Stories of men who never returned to the villages but still feel guilt. Stories of women who hold their families together but collapse in private. Stories of people who believe that their wealth is proof of healing—but whose emotional wounds tell another story.

To help others, we must help ourselves first. And to help ourselves, we must go back—not to the poverty or the pain—but to the parts of us that never received the safety and attention they deserved. That is the invitation of therapy. That is the possibility of healing, even for the ones who seem to have it all.

7. When Money Tries to Hold What Love Couldn't

There are people who rise out of the dust with fire in their eyes. They come from homes where the fridge was always empty and the silence always loud. They learned not to ask for too much because "too much" was never there. Instead, they grew up in survival mode — loving from a distance, hoping from a crack in the window, and learning that tenderness was either absent or unpredictable.

And then they made it.

They worked harder than anyone else did. They pushed themselves through school, skipped meals to save money, started businesses with borrowed dreams, and they finally found it: economic success. The bank account started growing. The house back in the village was renovated. They sent money home. They bought the clothes they never had. The shoes. The car. The dignity that poverty once stole.

But deep inside, something remained a hunger no amount of money could satisfy.

Childhood Without Love Leaves Adult Confusion

Thabiso, a 36-year-old woman from Ga-Mphahlele, grew up with a father who drank and a mother who prayed silently with bruised arms. She was never hugged. Never told, "I love you." She was told to be strong. To behave. To survive.

When she made her first R50,000 from a tender project in Polokwane, she wept. Not because she was proud — but because it was the first time she felt *worthy*. Money became her apology to herself. She would never go hungry again. She would never beg anyone again. She would be her own provider, her own lover, her own miracle.

And yet, in every romantic relationship, she struggled. She bought her partners gifts. She paid rent. She offered her wallet when they needed a hand. But what she longed for most — true intimacy, gentleness, being held without conditions — always felt just out of reach.

Because money cannot hold you in the middle of the night. Money cannot speak the words you never heard as a child. Moreover, success, no matter how loud, cannot drown out the sound of a broken heart that never learned to trust.

When Love Becomes a Transaction

Many who come from broken, economically unstable backgrounds begin to confuse generosity with love.

They assume:

- If I pay your tuition, you must stay.
- If I bought you food, you should not complain.
- If I gave you everything I never had, why do I still feel unloved?

However, love is not a receipt. It cannot be calculated. It cannot be stored in a bank.

Nare sat quietly on the wooden bench outside the clinic in Mankweng. It was not a hospital—not quite. But inside, people sat in soft chairs and talked about things she had only ever whispered to herself in the dark. They called it "therapy." She wasn't sure what that word meant in her world, but she was tired. Tired of fighting with people who loved her. Tired of giving too much. Tired of never being understood.

She clenched the folded paper in her hand — the one with her name and the appointment time scribbled in blue ink. A man walked past. He glanced at her. She looked away. She didn't want anyone from the village to see her. Therapy was for the mad, they said. But she wasn't mad. She was just... sad.

When her name was called, she stood as if her body weighed more than it should. Every step into that room felt like trespassing into a world she didn't belong to.

THE HEALING WE NEVER SPOKE OF: THERAPY

The therapist was a woman. Older. Calm. There was a green curtain on the window that fluttered slightly with the wind. The smell of tea drifted from a cup on the desk.

"Welcome, Nare," the woman said gently. "You made it."

She nodded. "I almost didn't come."

"But you did."

Nare stared at her hands. She wanted to say everything and nothing at the same time. Her voice trembled when it finally came.

"I fight with people. I give too much. I... I don't know what's wrong with me."

The therapist didn't interrupt. She didn't write anything. She just listened.

"I come from a family that had nothing," Nare said, more slowly now. "My mother used to cry while peeling potatoes. My father left before I was born. I've worked so hard. Got a degree. A job. I even built her a house back home."

"Your mother?"

She nodded. "But she still says I'm distant. Cold. That I don't care. And my boyfriend says the same. He says I don't trust him. That I try to control everything."

"Do you?"

"I think I do. I don't mean to. I just... I panic when I feel I'm losing someone. So I overcompensate. I buy things. I fix things. I give more. Then I resent them when they don't love me back the way I expect."

The room grew quiet. Outside, a bird chirped from the tree nearby.

"Do you know," the therapist said softly, "sometimes we mistake performance for love. When we grow up in survival, love becomes something we *do*, not something we *are*."

"I don't know how to just... be loved."

"That's why you're here."

Nare looked up. Her eyes glistened, but she wasn't crying yet. It was too early for tears. But something inside her had shifted. Just a little. A corner of herself—one she never dared touch—had heard its own name.

Over the next few weeks, she returned. Every Wednesday afternoon.

And little by little, the truth came out.

How her first boyfriend left her after she paid his rent.

How she begged her mother to say "I'm proud of you," but never heard it.

How she felt guilty for success.

How she feared that if she stopped giving, no one would stay.

The therapist never judged. She never said "you should." She just asked questions like:

- "What does love mean to you?"
- "What do you think happens if you stop fixing everyone else?"
- "What would peace of mind look like for you?"

THE HEALING WE NEVER SPOKE OF: THERAPY

In that small room with the green curtain, Nare began to unlearn the stories she was taught in her childhood — that love was earned, that vulnerability was weakness, that she must do everything alone.

She started to understand that **control** was her armor. That **resentment** was her body's way of saying "I gave too much without receiving." That emotional misunderstanding came from never being taught how to speak the language of her own heart.

One afternoon, she arrived and told the therapist something new.

"I told my boyfriend I needed space," she said.

The therapist raised an eyebrow.

"I didn't say it to punish him. I said it because I want to learn to breathe alone. To choose love, not to chase it."

The therapist smiled.

"And how did it feel?"

"Terrifying. And free."

Peace of mind doesn't come like a waterfall. It comes like a soft, steady drip that wears away the stone. For Nare, therapy was not magic. It was a mirror. A quiet space where her survival could transform into self-awareness.

And in that awareness, her heart found a new kind of rhythm — not the pounding of fear, but the gentle drumbeat of healing.

A woman who only knows how to show love through sacrifice may exhaust herself trying to be enough. A man who thinks love is about provision may go numb when his partner wants presence, not presents.

And when they are rejected — when the money is not enough — they do not understand that the pain they feel is not just rejection of their love, but the reopening of an old wound: the childhood pain of not being enough without performing.

Healing begins when we stop assuming that financial success equals emotional healing.

A man from Jane Furse who grew up in a shack without electricity once said, "Now that I've built a double-story house, why do I still feel like a boy when my wife shouts at me?"

The answer lies in what was never given in his youth: emotional affirmation, safe love, affection, healthy communication. Money didn't fail him. Childhood did.

So, those who try to replace love with money must begin to ask — not assume:

- "What do I need emotionally?"
- "Am I buying this to feel loved, or to avoid feeling unworthy?"
- "Do I understand love without conditions?"
- "Have I allowed myself to grieve my childhood?"

Therapy — especially culturally sensitive psychoanalysis — can help make space for these questions. For a man to sit with a therapist in a clinic in Tzaneen or a community hall in Bolobedu and admit, "I don't know how to be loved without giving something in return," is the beginning of freedom.

Let us be clear: there is no shame in working hard. There is no shame in wanting comfort after years of hardship. Money can bring ease, choice, dignity, and respect.

But money is not love.

It cannot unteach the belief that you are unlovable. It cannot replace the embrace you never received. It cannot teach you how to stay present in a relationship, or how to trust someone when all you know is betrayal.

The people who rise from poverty must not only learn how to earn — but how to feel. How to ask. How to receive. How to heal.

What would happen if the next generation did not only inherit land, livestock, and bank accounts — but also **emotional literacy**?

What if a daughter from Mankweng was told, "You deserve love even when you are not useful"?

What if a son from Giyani heard, "Your vulnerability is not weakness — it is truth"?

This is the new wealth we must seek.

Because healing is not about escaping the past. It is about facing it, gently, with tools money cannot buy — but the heart deeply craves.

This is the quiet truth of many women who have moved to cities, but carry the village inside their bones.

Healing, for her, may not start in the therapist's office. It may begin in a moment of reflection at a funeral. Or a breakdown in her car on the way home from work. Or in a song from home that suddenly makes her sob in the supermarket.

And if she does walk into therapy, what she needs is not analysis first—but affirmation.

Not a solution—but a safe space.

Not a diagnosis—but a chance to be seen beyond her strength.

Because when she says, *"I'm just tired,"* she may really be saying,

"I've been holding too much for too long. And I don't know how to begin."

They must also actively work to create **safe, confidential spaces** where women feel empowered to speak freely. Community outreach, peer support groups, and integrating therapy into existing women's programs (such as literacy classes or maternal health services) can be powerful entry points. Additionally, involving female community leaders or health workers as trusted intermediaries can help bridge the gap between women and therapy services.

8. Hidden Wounds – Ferenczi, Jung, and the Burden of Rural Silence

In a village called Ga-Matlala, the wind moves slowly, as if it, too, is tired from carrying the weight of unspoken things.

A young boy, no more than eleven, hasn't spoken in days. His mother thinks he is bewitched. The sangoma says the ancestors are quiet around him, and that means something is not yet ready. The nurse at the clinic suspects trauma, but the file says only: *"headaches and sleep disturbance."*

No one says the word depression. It's too foreign. Too heavy.

But the pain is here. It walks in the dusty streets. It sits behind school desks. It cooks meals. It sings at funerals.

Ferenczi in the Fields – The Need to Be Believed

Sándor Ferenczi, one of Freud's most daring students, broke from his teacher in one crucial way: he believed trauma is real, not imagined.

While Freud backed away from the idea that early abuse could cause lasting neurosis, Ferenczi moved deeper into the child's inner world. He insisted on listening to the truth—even when the truth was uncomfortable.

"The child is often punished not for lying, but for telling the truth," he once said.

In rural settings, this rings painfully true.

Children who cry too much are labeled "attention seekers."

Women who speak of abuse are called "ungrateful."

Men who feel sadness are told to "man up."

Ferenczi would not have asked them to repress.

He would have said: *"Tell me what happened. And I will believe you."*

In these settings, the greatest gift therapy can offer is not advice—but attunement.

"I see you."

"You are not mad."

"You make sense."

This is what Ferenczi called mutuality—a deep, shared understanding that what hurts can heal if it is finally allowed to be spoken.

Jung in the Hills – Listening to the Soul of the Village

Carl Jung would have approached the suffering of these communities with reverence.

He understood that the soul of a person is never separate from the soul of their culture. He believed that symbols, myths, and archetypes live not just in books—but in people's dreams, rituals, and illnesses.

If Jung were in Mokopane, walking the footpaths between homes, he would not ask immediately for symptoms. He would ask:

"What do you dream of at night?"

"What stories did your grandfather tell?"

"When did the spirit of joy leave your house?"

Jung believed that what appears as depression is often a soul's rebellion—a cry for attention, meaning, or transformation.

In rural villages, where dreams are sacred and ancestors speak in silence, Jung would listen carefully. He would not rush to label.

Instead, he might say:

"Perhaps your sadness is a message. Let us listen to it together."

Where Ferenczi focused on the reality of relational trauma, Jung opened the door to collective trauma—the wounds passed down through history, through colonization, through silence.

Rural communities face a quiet epidemic.

- Depression that looks like fatigue or withdrawal.

Healing Bolobedu Through the Language of Therapy

The mornings in **Bolobedu** begin early, long before the sun has fully stretched across the maize fields. Roosters crow. Pots clatter. Life stirs. But beneath the surface of this beautiful, rhythmic existence is a silence so heavy it can't be swept away with the morning dust.

In one of the small, worn-down houses with a tin roof and a single mango tree in the yard, **MmaKgomotso** sits alone. Her husband works in Johannesburg, like many others. He visits once a month, sometimes less. He sends money when he can. He sends silence when he can't.

What he doesn't know is that his absence has become her grief. And grief, when unspoken, doesn't just sit quietly. It sinks—into the chest, into the bones, into the sleep, into the soul.

She doesn't call it depression. She calls it "tiredness."

She doesn't say she's anxious. She says, "I don't sleep well."

She goes to the clinic sometimes. They check her blood pressure. They give her pills for pain.

But the pain isn't in her body.

It's in the space between who she is and who she can talk to.

The Village Epidemic No One Talks About

In Bolobedu, and many places across Limpopo, depression wears many masks:

- A young wife who no longer sings while washing clothes.
- A polygamous household where wives share space but not sorrow.
- A teenage boy who dropped out of school after his father left for Johannesburg and never returned.
- A grandmother raising five children on a grant, with nothing but faith and fatigue.

The therapist and filmmaker **Branny Mthelebofu** came into this space not with a camera first—but with questions.

"What if this isn't just culture? What if this is silent suffering?"

"What if therapy could help, not by changing the people—but by giving them language for what hurts?"

Branny didn't want to pathologize tradition. She didn't want to erase culture.

She wanted to listen differently.

What Therapy Can Offer Bolobedu

Therapy, in its true form, is not about "fixing" broken people. It is about **restoring the voice** that trauma has silenced.

Restoring Broken Marriages

In long-distance relationships, especially common in Limpopo's villages, men work far away, and women stay behind. Over time, connection becomes currency, and intimacy is replaced by obligation.

Therapy can create a bridge:

- A space where couples can speak honestly about loneliness without blame.

- A place where silence is not a punishment but a question: *"What are we really afraid to say?"*
- A process that helps husbands and wives find their way back to each other—not just physically, but emotionally.

Branny once facilitated a session between a young wife and her absent husband. The man, hardened by years of city labor, began the session in defense.

By the end, he wept like a child.

"I thought I was building our future," he said.

"But I didn't see that I was breaking our now."

This wasn't failure. It was **healing**.

Reframing Polygamy and Women's Silence

In polygamous homes, the unspoken becomes a third partner in the marriage. Women are taught to endure, not express. To sacrifice, not share.

Therapy does not aim to dissolve polygamy—it asks: *"How are your hearts doing in this arrangement?"*

In a women's therapy circle Branny helped initiate, one of the elder wives said:

"We all have our own plates in the kitchen, but no one knows the hunger inside the other's stomach."

They began to speak—not to accuse, but to be seen.

Sometimes, that is all the body has been asking for.

THE HEALING WE NEVER SPOKE OF: THERAPY

The children of Bolobedu carry more than schoolbags. They carry the emotional gaps of absent fathers, anxious mothers, and exhausted grandmothers.

Psychoanalysis calls this inherited affect—feelings passed down not through blood, but through silence, stress, and sorrow.

In Branny's work with children, therapy looked like play. Like drawing. Like stories about "invisible friends" who were actually expressions of fear and longing.

One child drew a picture of a house with no windows.

"Why no windows?" Branny asked.

"Because nobody sees us," the boy replied.

Therapy made that child visible—for the first time.

Because the villagers don't understand anxiety, they don't seek the help of a psychoanalyst. Branny Mthelebofu has been wondering why many people experience stomach pains after attending funerals and why they don't know the cause. Many people have berried their pains, and during community funerals, particularly in the villages, suffering occurs silently as they bury their siblings. In the townships and villages in the province of Limpopo, as well as other rural areas in South Africa, we have seen numerous widows, both young and old, who have never gone to therapy after losing their partners.

Carl Jun claims that attending funerals causes them grief. Perhaps this needs more discussion, but in a rural setting, the filmmakers attempt to depict their suffering through TV or short films.

Therapy in Bolobedu must speak more than English.

It must speak **Sepedi, Xitsonga, Tshivenda.**

It must speak praise poetry and proverbs, ritual and rhythm, firelight and fellowship.

Branny helped adapt sessions that opened with prayer, and closed with song.

She worked with elders, not against them.

She invited traditional healers into conversation, not competition.

Therapy here was not an outsider's intervention.

It was an insider's remembering—a way to come home to the parts of themselves the villagers had long buried under duty, tradition, and resilience.

When Branny walks through the dusty paths of Bolobedu, people greet her not just as a filmmaker or therapist—but as someone who brings a new kind of mirror.

A mirror that says:

- *You do not have to be strong all the time.*
- *Your feelings are not curses.*
- *Your tears do not dishonor your family.*
- *You can speak, and you will be heard.*

Therapy does not replace tradition.

It **wakes up** the person inside it.

And for villages like Bolobedu, maybe that is the healing they've been waiting for all along.

- **Anxiety** that shows up as stomach pain.

When Anxiety Has No Name in the Village

In the heart of **Limpopo Province**, where the air tastes of dust and tradition, the villagers know how to bury their dead.

What they don't know is how to bury their pain—or even name it.

A funeral in the village is not just a ritual; it is a collective confrontation with memory. The singing, the kneeling, the procession, the grave—each gesture wrapped in dignity. But when the final prayer is said and the last handful of soil falls on the casket, something else lingers.

The body speaks what the mouth cannot.

Branny Mthelebofu, a therapist and filmmaker born of these same soil-paths and mango trees, started noticing something odd.

"Why is everyone complaining of diarrhea after funerals?" she asked one of the nurses at the local clinic.

The answer was vague. "Maybe it's the food," someone offered.

But Branny wasn't convinced. She wasn't just looking with medical eyes—she was listening with emotional ears.

And what she heard was silence.

"We've buried too many people without ever burying the pain that came with them,"

Branny would later say in a short film titled *"The Gut That Remembers."*

Women wept with swollen eyes. Men clenched their jaws in control.

But their bodies—especially their stomachs—betrayed them.

Carl Jung: The Shadow That Returns

If Carl Jung had walked the footpaths of Ga-Mokopane or Bolobedu, he would have recognized it immediately: The Shadow.

In Jungian theory, the shadow is the part of ourselves that we repress—our pain, grief, vulnerability, rage. It lives behind our public masks. In the rural villages of South Africa, that mask is thickened by tradition, by respect, by silence.

And so, when villagers attend funerals, especially of siblings or partners long lost, the shadow rises. Not in words—but in symptoms.

Jung once said, *"Until you make the unconscious conscious, it will direct your life and you will call it fate."*

In the villages, they don't call it anxiety.

They call it **"diarrea ya dipoko"** — the ghost's stomach.

They call it **"stress ya matshwenyego"** — stress of troubles.

But they never call it what it often is: grief without voice.

In every funeral, Branny noticed a familiar face.

Women draped in black, eyes dry not because they didn't feel—but because they had cried too many times in private.

The older widows whispered only in kitchens.

The younger ones stayed home, not wanting to be seen.

None had been to therapy.

One woman told Branny: *"I did not only bury my husband. I buried my dreams. I buried the woman I was before he died."*

But what happens when dreams rot inside the soul?

The body finds a way to purge them—sometimes through anxiety, sometimes through illness.

Sometimes through stomach pain that no pill can reach.

Anxiety in the Language of the Body

In the villages, anxiety doesn't speak in psychological terms.

There is no word in Sepedi or Tshivenda that captures "panic attack."

There is no clean translation for "generalized anxiety disorder."

Instead, anxiety becomes:

A rural lady who has never had the freedom to express her feelings can never comprehend these terms in a session, so how can someone who needs more understanding in South Africa's communities go about their journey?

Anxiety instead manifests as: A shaky hand at night, a weight on the chest, and an unsettling stomach in addition to experiencing dyspnoea while listening to the funeral hymn.

In the villages of South Africa, especially in the quiet corners of Limpopo, Free State, and the Eastern Cape, many women have lived their entire lives being told to be strong. Strength has meant silence. It has meant cooking while grieving. It has meant carrying pain in the belly, and wiping tears without anyone seeing.

But what happens when a woman has no space to speak about what hurts her?

What happens when she grows up being told, *"Re kga mpya – we don't talk about feelings"* or *"Be grateful; other people have it worse"*?

She learns to bury her pain so deeply that she doesn't even know it's there anymore.

Yet, the body remembers.

n many therapy rooms in the cities, the word "**anxiety**" is used often. But in the villages, that word does not always land. To a rural woman, it is just a big word that sounds like something for "people in town."

But she *knows* the feeling—she just calls it something else.

It is the weight on her chest when she hears a hymn being sung at a funeral.

It is the stomach that won't settle, no matter how much ginger tea she drinks.

It is the shaking of her hands at night, when memories come like wind through the cracks of an old house.

It is the shortness of breath, not from running, but from crying silently while everyone sings around her.

This, too, is anxiety.

This is the body's way of speaking when the mouth has been trained to keep quiet.

For a woman who has never spoken freely about her emotions, therapy can sound like a scary thing. A stranger asking about her feelings? What if she doesn't have the right words?

But therapy does not begin with big English words. It begins with a story. Sometimes even a song. Sometimes a simple sentence like:

THE HEALING WE NEVER SPOKE OF: THERAPY

"There are days when I feel tired, but not in my body—in my heart."

That is enough.

Therapy, when done with care and cultural understanding, doesn't ask a rural woman to leave her identity behind. It meets her exactly where she is.

She does not need to have all the answers.

She does not need to speak perfectly.

She only needs to begin with truth—her truth.

Here are small steps she can take:

1. Speak to a woman she trusts—a sister, a neighbor, or a community worker who has shown kindness. Sometimes healing begins with one safe person.
2. Attend a village women's circle or support group. If these don't exist, maybe she can help start one—with just tea, a bench under the tree, and honesty.
3. Listen to others tell their stories. When she hears that she's not alone, something in her heart might begin to soften.
4. Visit a culturally sensitive therapist—someone who respects her background, her language, her ways. Someone who knows that a proverb can say more than a diagnosis.

This woman, the one who has never had the freedom to talk about her emotions, is not sick. She is burdened. She is suffocating under years of unspoken sorrow.

A crying baby is comforted.

But who comforts the crying woman who never allowed herself to weep?

The therapy space, when done right, can become that comfort.

It will not erase her past.

But it will help her make peace with it.

And maybe, just maybe, the trembling in her hands will quiet.

The weight on her chest will lift.

And when the funeral hymn is sung again, she will be able to breathe.

Branny, with her camera and compassion, began to document this in her short films—real stories of widows, brothers, cousins, neighbors.

One film opened with a man vomiting in the bushes after a burial.

He says only: *"Ke a imelwa hle... something is sitting on me."*

It's not food poisoning. It's emotional indigestion.

The emotional indigestion about the lost of partners, or loosing someone that you love, especially now that when young men are leaving the village life to Gauteng Province, the City of Gold to look for more opportunities they break up with their partners and never return, now the women or men in the villages are living with trauma and end up in emotional indigestion that has no solution. The psychoanalysis therapy is supposed to assist these people in the village set up but will this affect their current romantic partners?

In the villages of Limpopo, where dust roads snake between koppies and goats still cross footpaths without haste, loss is not always marked by death. Sometimes, loss sounds like a cellphone that never rings again.

The young men—bright-eyed, restless, carrying dreams like duffel bags—leave for Gauteng, the City of Gold. The promise is always the same: *"Ke ya go bona tsela – I'm going to find a way."* But months become years. Years become silence.

Back in the village, someone waits.

And in the waiting, something breaks.

Not Death, but Abandonment

The kind of grief that fills the houses of Ga-Mokopane or Bolobedu is not dressed in black. It does not weep at graves. It stirs quietly, like smoke trapped inside a calabash.

When her fiancé never shows up, a lady waits for him in the hope that he will return but this creates more problems.

Numerous ladies wait for their fiancé who never comes back to the village. How does this affect their current relationship, and is there any chance that someone will be able to help them in this situation?

In a small village tucked between the dusty roads of Limpopo and the slow dance of the thorn trees, there lived a woman named MmaThandi. She had once been promised love beneath the low stars of a warm autumn sky. Her fiancé, Jabulani, had sworn to return after finding work in Johannesburg. He had held her hand tightly before boarding the bus at the crossroads, promising to come back by Christmas.

That was fifteen Christmases ago.

Every year, she cooked as if he would walk in. She washed the sheets in the small rondavel where they were supposed to live. She sat on the stoep in the evenings, watching the path he would take when he returned.

But he never did.

To the village, MmaThandi seemed fine. She attended funerals, wore dignified dresses to church, and sang with her head held high. But beneath that calm face was a wound that never bled. It was not the kind of grief that screams. It was the kind that whispers through the years, echoing inside a woman's chest like an unanswered call.

She tried to move on. Years later, she entered into another relationship. He was a kind man, Sipho, who helped her carry firewood and laughed with her softly under the trees.

But she never fully gave herself to him.

Every time he was late, her chest tightened.

Every time he went to town, she stared at the gate too long.

Every time he said, "I'll be back," she didn't believe him.

She wasn't angry. She was haunted.

The past had never left her—it had simply put on a new face.

MmaThandi's story is not rare in the villages. There are many women who have loved deeply and been left behind—not always because of betrayal, but because of life, poverty, distance, or death.

When a man leaves and never returns, part of the woman stays waiting. She may smile, she may farm, she may raise children—but the waiting becomes a second life she lives quietly in her thoughts.

Her new partner, no matter how gentle, often competes with a memory.

The question then becomes: *Is there hope for healing?*

A therapist visiting the village once said to her, "You never let yourself grieve what you lost. You've been waiting for Jabulani to walk back into your yard—but you never gave yourself permission to bury the dream."

Those words sat with her like heavy rain.

For the first time, she cried in front of someone. She told the story of the morning he left, how his hands trembled, how her father had warned her not to trust a city boy. She remembered the weight of her hope—and the silence that followed.

The therapist did not offer advice. She offered presence.

In time, MmaThandi began to write letters to Jabulani—letters she would never send. She began to speak his name aloud, not with bitterness, but with release. She told Sipho about her grief, not to excuse her distance, but to invite him into her truth.

Something in her began to soften.

What therapy can do—especially in a culturally sensitive village setting—is not to erase the past, but to help a woman reclaim herself from it.

She does not have to stop loving the man who never came back.

But she must learn to stop waiting at the gate.

MmaThandi did not stop cooking.

She did not stop singing.

But now she did it for herself.

And when Sipho looked at her, she finally looked back—fully present.

Because healing, even in the rural silence of the villages, is not a foreign thing.

It is the act of saying:

"Yes, I was hurt."

"Yes, I waited."

"Yes, I am still here."

Letters to Someone Who Isn't Coming Back

In a quiet village where the wind speaks more than the people do, a man named Thapelo sits by the paraffin lamp every Sunday evening. The house is quiet except for the steady sound of a pen scratching paper. The children have fallen asleep. The maize meal pot has cooled. And Thapelo, once a man of few words, now writes what he never learned to say out loud.

The letters are always addressed the same way:

To my wife, Naledi, in Pretoria.

He writes about how the garden is growing. About how the borehole was dry last week. He tells her how little Ayanda lost her first tooth and how Lebo asked to be plaited like the girls in the city.

He ends every letter the same:

"We miss you. I hope you are well. Call when you can."

But Naledi never calls.

And Thapelo never posts the letters.

He places them carefully inside a tin box under his bed, like prayers he cannot pray out loud.

Naledi left for Pretoria three years ago to find work as a domestic helper. At first, she called every Sunday. Then the calls came monthly. Then they stopped.

She never said goodbye.

She just became a silence that thickened with time.

Thapelo kept telling the children, "Your mother is working. She'll come home soon." But he no longer believes it himself. There are whispers—village people who say they saw her in Soweto, with a ring on her finger and a man who isn't Thapelo.

He doesn't hate her. He doesn't curse her.

He just aches in a way that has no name.

9. Emotional Indigestion: When Goodbye is Never Said

- Children Asking Questions That Have No Gentle Answers

On school mornings, little Lebo asks him, "Papa, when is Mama coming home?"

Thapelo smiles, even when it hurts.

He tells her, "Soon."

Because what else can a man say when the truth might break his child's heart?

How do you tell a child that their mother is never coming back?

That she started a new life without them?

That you, the one left behind, must now carry both your grief and theirs?

The younger one, Ayanda, no longer remembers her mother's voice. She clings tighter to her father's hand and draws family pictures with only three figures now.

Every letter Thapelo writes is not really for Naledi anymore.

They are for himself.

They are how he holds onto dignity in a world where men are not supposed to weep.

They are how he teaches his daughters that love does not always vanish, even when people do.

He cannot afford a therapist.

There is no mental health center in the village.

But in those pages, he begins to unravel the knots inside his chest.

He begins to forgive—her, and maybe even himself.

Love in the villages doesn't always look like happy endings.

Sometimes, it looks like a man waking early to braid his daughter's hair.

It looks like empty school chairs at parents' meetings, filled only by fathers who learned how to be both mother and father.

It looks like holding onto hope until you no longer need it to survive.

Will Naledi ever return?

No one knows.

But Thapelo has found something else—the strength to live even when someone you love chooses a different path.

People in the village notice. They always do.

But they do not mock him.

They greet him kindly at the spaza shop.

The older women sometimes bring him spinach from their gardens.

And the men, though they do not ask about Naledi, stand with him in quiet solidarity—because they, too, have known heartbreak they couldn't name.

THE HEALING WE NEVER SPOKE OF: THERAPY

If therapy were available in his village, Thapelo would be a candidate for healing. Not because he is weak, but **because** he has carried strength alone for too long.

And perhaps, one day, when his daughters are older and ask for the truth, he will show them the box of letters under the bed.

Not to shame their mother.

But to show them what love tried to be.

This is a different kind of mourning.

It is not for the dead.

It is for the living who left.

Villagers often complain of tight chests, upset stomachs, sleepless nights, weight loss, **or** numb limbs.

But when the nurses run tests, nothing is found. No virus. No bacteria. No parasite.

The illness is emotional indigestion.

Not of food—but of *unspoken pain*.

"I cannot eat. I feel full even when I am hungry," says Maria, 46, whose boyfriend left for Johannesburg twelve years ago.

"He promised he would come back. I still dream of him. I have never had another partner."

She pauses.

"My body is fine, but I am tired inside."

This tiredness does not heal with rest. It lives in the places that medicine cannot reach.

Psychoanalysis, if it ever hopes to work in these villages, must first listen. Not with pity, not with superiority, but with humility.

In the therapy room—or the rondavel, if it must be there—the conversation might begin with a story, not a symptom.

A patient might speak of goats not returning from the field.

But what they are truly talking about is their own sense of abandonment.

"He said he would come back after two months. That was 2009."

The psychoanalyst does not rush to interpret. They ask, *"And how has your heart lived since then?"*

Here, therapy becomes the place where unsaid goodbyes finally find their voices.

Romantic Ghosts in New Relationships

But what happens when a woman who was left behind falls in love again?

What if the man who lost his wife to the city tries to move on?

This is where psychoanalysis stirs more than healing—it stirs *truth*.

Unprocessed grief becomes a shadow in the new relationship.

The new partner feels compared.

They carry the burden of being *better than the one who left, more present than the one who vanished*, or *more faithful than the ghost they compete with*.

Therapy, in this context, is not a threat to current love.

It is a gift to it.

By digesting the past, one becomes emotionally available for the present.

Without it, love becomes performance—never fully lived.

A Session in the Village: Two Women and a Silence

In one women's circle in Bolobedu, hosted under a marula tree, two women spoke.

"My man left for Joburg in 2012. I hear he now has three children. I never moved on."

The other woman nodded. "Mine too. I started seeing someone else, but I don't love him. I just needed someone to hold me at night."

The therapist, sitting quietly with a notebook, asked:

"Did either of you ever get to say goodbye?"

They both shook their heads.

"Then your stomachs are full," the therapist said.

"Not with food. But with love that never had an ending."

Let the Goodbye Be Spoken

The body is wise.

It remembers every goodbye that was never given the dignity of words.

In Limpopo's rural communities, the migration of youth has left an emotional famine in the hearts of those who stay behind. Romantic loss that is never acknowledged becomes chronic tension, grief without closure, or indigestion that no herbal tea can ease.

Psychoanalysis offers not a cure, but a conversation.

Not an answer, but a question: *"Can we talk about what never had a name?"*

If given a chance, therapy in the villages could become a place where:

- Abandoned lovers mourn in dignity.
- New partners are welcomed with clear hearts.
- And no one must live with the ache of love turned into silence.

Because in the end, to grieve aloud is not to be weak.

It is to be human.

And to love again—not from emptiness, but from clarity.

10. Can Psychoanalysis Speak Sepedi?

This question haunted Branny as she sat in her editing room, re-watching footage of widows and mourners crumpling not from grief—but from the weight of unprocessed emotion.

Could psychoanalysis—born in Vienna, shaped by Freud and Jung—find a home in Limpopo's rural settings?

Yes, but it must adapt.

It must understand:

- That crying at therapy is seen as weakness here.

When Prayer Opens the Door to Psychoanalysis

In the rural folds of South Africa—where gravel roads remember every footstep and huts carry the scent of ancestral memory—healing is not a new concept. It is ancient. It is woven into song, embedded in customs, and whispered in twilight prayers. But what if this familiar terrain held space for a quiet visitor: the inner world of the unconscious mind?

What if hypnosis and psychoanalysis, tools often seen as Western and distant, could speak in the language of villages—not with prompts or jargon, but with prayer and proverbs?

Branny Mthelebofu, a filmmaker and a listener of stories, began asking these questions not in psychology textbooks, but in church benches, village circles, and fading kitchen light. He noticed something: villagers already practiced a kind of trance. They just didn't call it that.

When the old woman in Mokopane hums a hymn and stares into the fire, she enters a light trance.

When a young man kneels for hours praying for clarity about his life, he is suspended between consciousness and reflection.

When a grieving mother dreams of her child and believes she has received a message from the spirit world, she is processing, integrating, understanding—through symbols.

What psychoanalysis calls the unconscious, villagers often experience as spirit.

What therapists might call "hypnotic suggestion," villagers experience as a prayer received.

And what psychologists term "suppressed memory," rural elders call a story swallowed by silence.

There is no conflict here.

Only a mistranslation.

In the imagined therapy huts Branny sees one day flourishing across Limpopo, the session never begins with "Tell me your trauma." That would be a breach of emotional protocol. No, in this space, the session might begin with:

"Mmago ngwana o swara thipa ka bogaleng."

"A mother holds the knife by the blade."

The proverb lands. The woman nods slowly. She knows what this means. She knows the pain, the silence, the sacrifice. Her body relaxes—because her culture has been invited in.

From there, the therapist or healer might say, "Tell me about the knife you've been holding."

Hypnosis, the Rural Way

Hypnosis doesn't need to look like swinging clocks or unfamiliar voices. In the village, it might look like:

- Sitting quietly under a tree with a trusted elder, eyes closed, remembering what was once buried.
- Listening to a soft drum beat, a hymn, or the rustle of wind—until the conscious mind quiets.
- Following a guided narrative told in metaphor: *"Imagine you are walking through your grandmother's garden. What do you see there? What has been left behind?"*

In this state of deep relaxation—anchored in trust and story—a woman may revisit the night her husband left and never came back. A man may face the child he lost but never mourned. These are not tricks. These are truths waiting to rise.

And when they do, the prayer returns—not to cover the pain, but to bless the courage of naming it.

Many villagers may not ask for hypnosis or psychoanalysis by name. But they know suffering. They know insomnia that lasts years. Chest pain that no doctor can diagnose. Headaches that come only on the birthday of someone they lost.

They do not need to be convinced of their pain.

What they need is a path that honors their way of speaking. They need a therapist who can listen between silences. Who understands that a proverb is a confession. That a hymn is a cry. That tears are not weakness—but ancestral water washing pain.

In such spaces, hypnosis becomes familiar. Psychoanalysis becomes storytelling. Healing becomes possible.

The session closes not with advice, but with presence. Sometimes, a prayer is offered—not to bypass therapy, but to complete it.

"Molimo, o re bontshe moo bohloko bo iphitlhile teng."

"God, show us where the pain is hiding."

And as the prayer lifts into the air, the healing continues in the heart.

- That women are taught to carry pain like a badge of honor.
- That a man who shows vulnerability is "not strong enough."

But psychoanalysis also teaches something the villagers desperately need:

"The things we don't speak about speak through us anyway."

And in Limpopo, they often speak through the gut.

In one of Branny's experimental community group sessions, she asked the group what their bodies do at funerals.

A middle-aged man raised his hand.

"My stomach turns, every time. Since my brother died."

Branny asked gently, *"Did you ever talk about that loss with anyone?"*

He looked down. *"No. We don't talk like that at home. We just slaughter a goat and keep quiet."*

That silence, Branny told him later, wasn't his fault.

It was the system's inheritance.

But he could be the one to break it.

Where Prayer Meets Psychoanalysis – Branny Mthelebofu's Vision for Limpopo

Branny Mthelebofu was not trained as a psychologist. He was not a traditional healer either. But he was a listener—a filmmaker born in the heart of Limpopo Province, who spent years behind the lens documenting stories that no one had the language to name. It was in the quiet pauses between interviews, in the trembling voices of elders and the heavy sighs of widows, that Branny began to realize something profound: healing in the villages was not absent—it was hidden in plain sight.

In Limpopo, pain rarely enters the room alone. It walks with song, cloaked in silence, cloaked in prayer.

What Branny witnessed was not a rejection of therapy, but rather a misalignment of language and rhythm. The therapy rooms he imagined did not have sterile white walls or abstract jargon. Instead, they had the scent of burning impepho, the hum of old hymns, and the slow unfolding of stories told in metaphor.

He began to ask himself: What if therapy didn't have to fight culture?

What if therapy could walk alongside it?

The Sacred Fusion: Therapy with Ritual and Prayer

In the villages of Limpopo—whether in Bolobedu, Ga-Matlala, or Mokopane—people have always known how to gather around suffering. They do so through ritual, prayer, and song. A mother does not tell you she is depressed; she sings a hymn with a crack in her voice. A man does not say he is broken; he begins to pray with a shaking hand, tears hidden behind the words. These are not avoidance strategies—they are languages of grief.

Branny saw that in these moments, the line between spiritual practice and emotional expression blurred. And it was in this very blurring **that** a new kind of therapeutic possibility began to emerge.

What if therapy sessions began with a prayer, not as a religious formality, but as a cultural anchor?

What if group therapy in a village circle opened with a song, where people's hearts remembered what their tongues could not say?

What if storytelling was not just catharsis, but psychoanalytic work in its own right—layered with symbols, repression, projection, and memory?

In one of Branny's workshops in Bolobedu, he brought together a small circle of women who had never attended therapy before. They were widows, single mothers, grandmothers raising their children's children. None of them used words like "trauma" or "depression." But when asked to open with a prayer, their voices filled the room like a rising river.

After the prayer, one woman spoke:

"I've never cried in front of my children. I didn't know how to say that I'm tired."

Another followed:

"When my husband died, they said I must be strong. But inside, something broke, and I've never picked up the pieces."

They did not need coaxing.

They needed permission.

Permission to feel.

Permission to speak.

Permission to be more than what survival had forced them to become.

Branny saw it firsthand: prayer was not separate from therapy. It was the door to it.

Building a Model for Limpopo

Branny now envisions a model of psycho-social support deeply embedded in cultural practice:

Therapy sessions led by culturally fluent facilitators, who speak **Sepedi, Xitsonga, Tshivenda, or Setswana**—not just in language, but in emotional tone.

Sessions opened with traditional proverbs, grounding the conversation in wisdom passed down through generations.

Healing circles that honor spiritual rhythm—with music, memory, and meaning braided into every step.

Community elders and church leaders as allies, not adversaries, in the process of healing.

- Narrative therapy as storytelling, where people reconstruct their identities and rewrite their lives with dignity.

This is not about replacing psychology with prayer, or therapy with tradition. It's about integration. It's about meeting people where they are, so they can walk toward where they want to be.

In Limpopo Province, healing is not only about medicine or talk therapy. It is about restoring spiritual balance, finding voice in silence, and allowing people to tell their story in their own way.

And as Branny Mthelebofu continues his work—whether through film, community workshops, or dialogues with professionals—he carries one deep belief:

Therapy is not foreign. Pain is not new.

Only the bridges between them need to be rebuilt.

The Filmmaker's Fight Against Invisible Pain

Branny's films are now more than stories. They are medicine.

Played in churches, schools, clinics. They spark conversation.

They make villagers say:

"Wait... maybe it's not just my body. Maybe my heart is sick too."

She doesn't push therapy on anyone.

She invites them to see themselves—then make a choice.

One widow, after watching a short film about grief, whispered:

"Ke ntse ke sa tsebe gore ke lapa la pelo. I didn't know my heart was tired."

In Limpopo's villages, anxiety may never be called by its Western name.

But it is lived. It is felt. It is buried—then unearthed again at every funeral, with every song of goodbye.

Therapy, especially psychoanalysis, can help the villagers speak what has been stored for too long.

And through storytellers like Branny Mthelebofu, the camera becomes a mirror.

A tool to say:

"What you are feeling is real.

It is not shame.

It is not weakness.

It is a soul asking to be seen."

And maybe, finally, the village will listen.

- Substance abuse that masks grief and hopelessness.
- Suicide that no one wants to name.

These communities have few therapists. Few clinics.

But even more troubling: they have few listeners.

Ferenczi and Jung both understood that isolation is not just physical—it is emotional.

How, then, can psychoanalysis—this deep, often slow process—live in a fast-breaking, under-resourced village?

It must adapt, not dilute.

It must bend toward the people, not ask them to contort to theory.

Here is what this could look like:

Instead of trying to "fix" the villager who is depressed, the psychoanalyst listens like Ferenczi—gently, reverently. She does not assume the story is imagined or exaggerated. She accepts the pain as real.

THE HEALING WE NEVER SPOKE OF: THERAPY

A girl who stops eating is not defiant.

She is trying to control the only thing left to her—her hunger.

Instead of imposing diagnoses, the psychoanalyst invites the language of the people. As Jung would, she honors dreams, symbols, and traditions.

A man who dreams of rivers may not need pills.

He may need someone to ask what the water means in his life.

Group sessions under trees, in church halls, or homes allow for shared witnessing—what Ferenczi believed could repair relational trauma.

When a woman tells her story and another says, "Me too,"

that is the beginning of freedom.

The barriers are real:

- Stigma: "Therapy is for the weak."
- Access: "There is no clinic nearby."
- Language: "Will they understand my dialect?"
- Tradition: "Shouldn't we just pray or go to the healer?"

But so are the bridges:

- Trusted local facilitators trained in psychoanalysis-informed practices
- Culturally adapted tools using song, proverbs, and storytelling
- Mobile therapy sessions in local languages
- Partnerships between healers and therapists, not opposition

Ferenczi taught us to believe the wounded.

Jung taught us to listen to the soul, even when it speaks in myth.

And both, in their own ways, pointed toward this truth:

That healing comes not from silence, but from safe speech.

Not from labels, but from meaning.

Not from experts who "know," but from witnesses who care.

In rural settings, depression is not just a chemical imbalance.

It is often a story waiting to be heard.

And psychoanalysis, when translated through empathy, humility, and cultural fluency, can become not just therapy—but a return home to the self.

Holistic Therapy and the Challenge of Limited Healthcare Access

In many rural areas, basic healthcare services are either unavailable or under-resourced. Mental health support is often viewed as a luxury, far removed from the daily struggle for food, water, and physical health. This scarcity forces families to prioritize immediate survival over emotional wellbeing, leaving little room for therapy.

To address this, therapy must not stand alone—it must become part of a holistic approach to rural health. This means integrating mental health support into existing primary care centers, schools, agricultural extension services, and even religious institutions. By training local health workers and community volunteers in basic counseling and mental health first aid, we can create a decentralized model of care that reaches more people. Therapists, in turn, can rotate through communities, offering group sessions, workshops, or one-on-one support in a way that complements local customs and structures.

Breaking the Stigma: Cultural Sensitivity as a Key to Mental Health Acceptance

Perhaps the most difficult challenge is the stigma surrounding mental health. In many rural cultures, emotional suffering is viewed as weakness, punishment, or even spiritual failure. Those who seek therapy may be labeled as "mad" or "possessed," and families often discourage individuals from speaking to outsiders about personal problems.

To overcome this, therapists must approach communities with humility and cultural respect. Rather than imposing a clinical or Western model of therapy, they should seek to understand local beliefs about health, emotion, and healing. Cultural sensitivity in therapy involves using local languages, incorporating traditional practices when appropriate, and building relationships over time. Mental health must be reframed not as a diagnosis, but as a journey toward inner peace, balance, and resilience, values that often resonate deeply in village life.

Community education campaigns—led by local role models, educators, or even storytellers—can help reframe therapy as a strength, not a weakness. When people hear stories that reflect their own struggles, and see others seeking help and improving their lives, the stigma begins to lift.

The road to expanding therapy services in rural areas is not easy. It demands patience, empathy, and deep cultural understanding. Yet the rewards are immense. When women find their voices, when healthcare becomes truly holistic, and when stigma is replaced with compassion, communities transform. Therapy, then, becomes not just a service, but a catalyst for healing, dignity, and empowerment in places that have too long been forgotten.

11. Why Women Keep Their Feelings Hidden in Rural Villages

In the quiet corners of rural villages, far from the noise and bustle of cities, a different kind of silence reigns. It is not the peaceful quiet of nature or simplicity, but the silence of suppressed emotion, buried pain, and unspoken stories. Across these communities, women carry heavy emotional burdens in silence—trapped not only by external limitations but by an inherited culture of endurance. Despite the growing recognition of mental health needs in rural areas, the emotional worlds of women often remain invisible, locked behind closed doors and within guarded hearts.

From a young age, girls in rural villages are taught the value of endurance. They are told to be strong, to bear pain without complaint, and to place the needs of others before their own. This cultural script, passed down through generations, glorifies the suffering woman—the silent mother, the obedient daughter, the selfless wife. Expressing personal feelings is often seen as selfish or even shameful.

In many traditional settings, emotional expression is gendered. While men may be permitted to express anger or frustration, women are expected to maintain composure, obedience, and modesty. A crying woman is "weak"; a complaining woman is "ungrateful." Over time, women internalize these messages and begin to suppress their emotions, believing that silence is the price of respect and belonging.

In the hills beyond Mokopane, among villages sewn together by gravel roads and gossip passed between clotheslines, women carry stories in their backs.

THE HEALING WE NEVER SPOKE OF: THERAPY

They bend to fetch water, lift babies, and prepare firewood—but the weight they carry is not always visible. It lives beneath the skin, in sighs held too long, in words swallowed before they could become sentences.

Here, emotional expression is a matter of culture—and of gender.

Men can shout.

Men can leave.

Men can throw fists or slam doors, and no one calls them weak.

But women? Women must remain composed.

A crying woman is "unstable."

A complaining woman is "ungrateful."

An angry woman is "disrespectful."

And so, they learn early.

At their mother's knee, they hear it whispered:

"Be strong. Don't shame the family."

At church, they are taught:

"A good woman is patient. Quiet. Long-suffering."

At home, they live it.

The uncle who drinks too much. The father who forgets birthdays. The husband who returns home smelling of another woman's perfume. And through it all—she smiles. Or at least, she doesn't cry in public.

It is no wonder then, that silence becomes the native tongue of survival.

One woman—Letta, from a village near Ga-Molekana—once described it like this:

"I became two people. The one who cooks and laughs with neighbors. And the one who cries into a dishcloth while no one is watching."

Psychoanalysis calls this *splitting*—a psychological coping mechanism in which a person divides the self into parts, separating acceptable feelings from the unacceptable. Letta's public self was composed. Her private self was crumbling.

Over time, the two selves grow further apart. And the woman forgets which one is real.

This is not madness. It is adaptation.

In a society where belonging is conditional, women trade emotional honesty for approval. They trade their voice for stability. And they learn to carry grief like jewelry—present but polished.

How Psychoanalysis Intervenes

Psychoanalysis does not scold this silence. It does not rush to break it apart. Instead, it **sits with it**. Listens to it. Asks:

- *"When did you first learn that crying was dangerous?"*
- *"Whose love did you fear losing if you spoke your truth?"*
- *"Where in your body do you feel your anger when you cannot speak it?"*

These are not questions that traditional settings usually allow. But they are questions that **heal the fracture between who a woman is and who she has been told to be**.

In therapy sessions, psychoanalysis provides something many village women have never had:

A room with no judgment.

A witness to their invisible wounds.

A mirror that says, *"You are not too much. You are not broken. You are simply unheard."*

Letta, after six months in therapy, remembered something she hadn't thought about in years. She was twelve, and had begun her first period. Scared, she cried. Her mother slapped her.

"Don't be dramatic. Every woman goes through it."

It was a small moment. But psychoanalysis teaches us that small moments often cast long shadows.

Letta learned that day that womanhood meant **carrying discomfort alone**. That her pain would not be met with comfort, but with correction.

That moment became the seed of her silence.

Now, as a grown woman and mother herself, she noticed her voice softening when she wanted to yell. She noticed her smile stiffening when she wanted to sob.

Psychoanalysis helped her trace the map of her repression—back to the first cut, the first dismissal, the first silence.

And slowly, she began to undo the stitching.

This is not to say psychoanalysis comes without challenge. In traditional spaces, the idea of speaking openly about your emotions—let alone your private traumas—is still viewed as disloyal, even dangerous.

Women have been called selfish for seeking therapy. Told they are being influenced by "Western ideas" or that they are airing dirty laundry. But healing is not betrayal. Therapy is not rebellion. It is **remembrance**—of a time before the silence began.

Psychoanalysis does not erase culture. It **reveals the places where culture has hurt**, and offers tools to soften the wounds.

In the villages of Mogalakwena, you will still find women laughing together at water taps, weaving each other's hair on Sunday afternoons, singing hymns in church.

But listen closely, and you will hear another song—a quieter one.

It is the sound of women beginning to trust their own tears.

The whisper of suppressed emotions turning into speech.

The return of voice to those who thought theirs was too much, or too dangerous, or too inconvenient to matter.

Psychoanalysis, in this context, is not a foreign invasion. It is **a gentle return to self.**

And as more women begin to speak—really speak—the silence that once choked the village begins to loosen its grip.

Because when a woman learns that her feelings are not a weakness but a guide, she becomes **not less traditional, but more whole**.

And that, perhaps, is the most radical healing of all.

The tight-knit nature of rural life can be both a comfort and a curse. Everyone knows everyone. Privacy is limited, and news travels fast. For women, the risk of being judged, gossiped about, or misunderstood often outweighs the benefit of sharing their feelings. A woman who confides in another may be seen as inviting pity, shame, or scandal. In many cases, what should be a moment of vulnerability turns into a social risk.

Therapy, if available, is often mistrusted or misunderstood. Speaking to a therapist can be misinterpreted as admitting to mental illness or family dysfunction—labels that carry lasting social consequences. As a result, many women prefer to suffer in silence rather than seek support that might draw unwanted attention or damage their family's reputation.

In urban settings, women may find support through community centers, women's groups, support circles, or even informal meetups. But in many villages, such safe spaces are rare or nonexistent. Religious or cultural institutions may not allow women the freedom to gather, and when they do, the focus is usually on duties, not emotional wellbeing.

Without a trusted environment to speak openly, many women have nowhere to turn. Even within their families, emotional support may be lacking. Husbands may be dismissive; in-laws may be critical; even other women, hardened by their own experiences, may urge silence rather than solidarity. As a result, the burden of unspoken emotion grows heavier with time.

When Silence Feels Safer

Over time, silence becomes a strategy—a way to avoid conflict, maintain harmony, or protect one's children. Many women convince themselves that their feelings are unimportant or that suffering is simply their fate.

In the quiet corners of many rural villages, there are women who carry entire worlds on their backs. They rise before the sun, bend over fields or fires, carry children, and hold families together with threadbare hands and unspoken strength. Their lives are filled with service, sacrifice, and silence.

They do not cry often—at least, not where anyone can see. They do not talk about the weight in their chest or the ache in their heart. They whisper their pain into the pillow or into prayer, or bury it so deep that even they begin to forget it is there.

These are women who have been taught—by tradition, by community, and sometimes by religion—that their **feelings are secondary**, or worse, dangerous. That to be a "good woman" is to endure. That sorrow is their portion. That complaining is a sin. That joy is for others.

So they tell themselves a lie—one so old it begins to sound like truth.

"I'm fine."

"This is just how life is for women."

"As long as the children are okay, I'm okay."

"There is no time for feelings."

And with every repetition, they shrink a little more. Not in body—but in spirit.

These women may laugh at weddings and sing at church, but many of them carry wounds that were never spoken. A childhood trauma. A loveless marriage. Years of emotional neglect. The loneliness of being surrounded by people, yet never truly heard.

Yet still, they keep going. Because stopping means looking inward. And looking inward means facing feelings they were never taught to name.

To these women, **suffering has become identity**. It is what they know. It is what was passed down. Their mothers did not speak of emotional needs. Their grandmothers bore their burdens in silence. And so they believe: *This is what it means to be a woman.*

What if a woman's feelings are not a weakness—but a guide? What if the tears she hides are not shameful—but sacred? What if emotional pain is not her fate—but a sign that something within her still longs to live fully?

This is where **holistic therapy** enters—not as something foreign or shameful, but as a gentle doorway back to herself.

Holistic therapy understands that a woman is more than just her mind or her duties. She is **a whole person**—with emotions, memories, spirit, body, and dreams. And all these parts deserve attention. All these parts deserve care.

In a therapy setting, a woman can say the things she has never said aloud:

"I am tired of pretending."

"I don't feel seen."

THE HEALING WE NEVER SPOKE OF: THERAPY

"I don't know who I am anymore."

And instead of being silenced, she is met with understanding. She is **heard**.

Many women in rural communities seek physical healing—herbs for headaches, prayers for protection, rest for their bodies. But what of the heart? What of the places in the soul that are sore from years of being overlooked?

Holistic therapy does not separate the emotional from the spiritual, the cultural from the personal. It respects tradition while gently challenging what harms. It says:

- *You can believe in God and still need emotional support.*
- *You can love your family and still take time to care for yourself.*
- *You can be strong and still have feelings.*

Herbs for the Head, Silence for the Heart – When Emotional Pain Hides in the Body

In many rural communities across the world, healing begins with the land. The soil, the roots, the leaves—all are sacred tools passed down through generations. A woman with a pounding head reaches for the trusted herb her mother once brewed. A man with tightness in his chest is told to rest under a tree, drink ginger tea, and let the earth do its work.

And often, the body does respond. The headache eases. The chest loosens. The dizziness fades. But for how long?

Because beneath these physical symptoms, there is often another story—a quieter one. A story that begins not in the muscles or the stomach, but in the heart, the mind, and the soul.

That woman's headache? It returns every few days, especially after arguments or long nights of worry.

That man's chest pain? It worsens when he thinks about the crops failing, or the family tensions he cannot speak of.

And yet, rarely will they say, *"I think I am depressed."* Rarely will they ask, *"Could this be stress?"*

Why?

Because in many villages, **emotional pain wears a physical mask**—and that mask is easier to treat than the truth it hides.

THE HEALING WE NEVER SPOKE OF: THERAPY

In cultures where emotional expression is discouraged, where silence is considered strength, and where mental health has no safe name, **the body becomes the voice.**

A man will not say he is anxious about providing for his family, but he will say his chest feels tight.

A woman will not admit she cries herself to sleep, but she will mention that her head won't stop hurting.

These complaints are met with compassion, because **physical pain is respected** in a way that emotional pain is not. One can ask for herbs, for prayers, even for rest—but to say "I am broken inside" feels too shameful, too vulnerable, too foreign.

And so, the pain goes underground. It becomes invisible to others—and eventually, even to oneself.

It is easy to assume that rural people simply "don't know" about depression or stress. But the truth is more complex.

Many do know—deeply and instinctively—that they are not well. That something inside them is "heavy," "blocked," "dark," or "tired of life." But they do not have the words. Or worse, **they fear what the words might cost.**

To say you are depressed may be seen as weakness. To say you are emotionally overwhelmed may be heard as dishonoring your family, your culture, or your faith. And so, the body takes the burden.

The headache becomes the story. The back pain becomes the language. The herbs become the solution.

But it is only part of the solution.

12. Traditional Healing as a Stumbling Block to Therapy

In the heart of many villages, where the footpaths twist between fields and firewood leans against doorways, there is a rhythm that has lived for generations. It is the rhythm of traditional healing—of herbs boiled in silence, of prayers whispered under the stars, of a healer's hand placed on a trembling chest.

It is sacred.

It is known.

It is trusted.

When a child grows withdrawn or a woman faints from unseen burdens, the family visits the elder or healer. They are told it is a spiritual attack, or a curse, or the result of broken cultural protocols. And so the rituals begin—smoke, chants, bitter roots, and sacred water.

Sometimes, healing comes.

But other times, the pain lingers. The child grows colder. The woman breaks further. And the family wonders: *What else could this be?*

Yet, therapy—especially psychotherapy or psychoanalysis—remains far outside the village imagination. It is something "from the city," something "for mad people," or something that "questions tradition." It sits on the edge of community life like an unwelcome guest.

And so, the wounds deepen.

When Tradition Becomes a Wall Instead of a Bridge

It is not wrong to honor traditional healing. These practices carry wisdom that modern medicine has only begun to understand. They are embedded with cultural memory, spiritual belief, and communal identity. But there is a quiet problem, too.

Sometimes, tradition becomes the only voice allowed to speak.

A boy who is traumatized by domestic violence is taken to a healer to chase away spirits, but no one asks what he has seen.

A girl who was sexually abused is cleansed in a ritual bath, but no one helps her speak the truth.

A husband and wife who no longer sleep under the same roof are told to sacrifice a goat—but never to look each other in the eyes and talk.

These are not failures of culture.

They are failures of silence.

Traditional healing, when it refuses to coexist with emotional truth, becomes a **stumbling block**—not because it is false, but because it is **incomplete**.

Can Psychoanalysis Work in the Village?

Psychoanalysis, with its roots in Western psychology, might seem like a poor fit for village life. It is quiet. It is long. It demands self-reflection, emotional language, and deep introspection—skills that many rural people have never been taught or allowed to explore.

But at its core, psychoanalysis is not about couches and cold rooms. It is about **listening beneath the surface**. It is about tracing the invisible thread from pain to memory, from behavior to belief. It is about uncovering how the past lives in the present—and how silence, once broken, can set generations free.

Can this work in a rural setting?

Yes—but only if it adapts.

In villages, psychoanalysis must remove its formal coat and sit in the courtyard. It must learn to speak in proverbs. It must listen not just to words, but to pauses, glances, and the way a woman stirs her pot while avoiding your eyes. It must be humble enough to sit beside tradition—not above it.

Imagine a therapist who begins by asking:

"When did the sadness first arrive in your family?"

"Who was not allowed to cry in your home?"

"What story do you tell yourself when you suffer?"

These questions, asked gently, become keys. And once the door opens, **what was once hidden behind tradition begins to rise to the light.**

THE HEALING WE NEVER SPOKE OF: THERAPY

Many family wounds in rural areas are passed down, unspoken. A father who never said "I'm sorry." A grandmother whose grief turned into control. A mother who buried her voice to keep peace in the home. And children, watching, learning, repeating.

Traditional healers may not always address these emotional patterns. But psychoanalytic approaches can. When done with cultural sensitivity, this work becomes revolutionary. It helps families:

- See how emotional pain is inherited.
- Understand why love can feel dangerous.
- Release guilt and shame that is not theirs to carry.
- Make peace with their past without dishonoring it.

This is not a rejection of tradition. It is the **fulfillment** of it. Because true healing—healing that lasts—is not just about removing the pain. It is about **understanding it**, owning it, and transforming it.

One day, perhaps, a traditional healer and a trained therapist will sit together on a woven mat, drinking tea. One speaks of ancestral ties and spirit balance. The other speaks of emotional trauma and family dynamics. And both will nod—slowly, respectfully—because **they are speaking about the same wound**, from different angles.

In that moment, something new begins. Not a war between science and culture, but a **partnership** for deeper healing.

And maybe, just maybe, a woman who has cried in secret for ten years will finally be able to say,

"It was not a curse. I was just never allowed to feel."

And a man who drinks alone at night will say,

"I carry my father's silence—and I am tired."

And the therapist will listen. And the healer will bless. And the family will breathe.

Because when therapy and tradition no longer compete, but **collaborate**, the village finds not only medicine—but meaning.

It was late afternoon in the village of Mbali, the sky softening into orange, and the air heavy with the scent of firewood and maize. The goats had quieted, the children were still, and in a shaded compound behind the clinic, two chairs were pulled beneath a tree.

One belonged to **Mama Khosi**, the village's respected healer—known for her hands, her herbs, and her gift of reading what others could not say. The other chair was for **Nora**, a soft-spoken therapist from the city who had been working gently in the community for several months, earning trust one family at a time.

Between them sat **Noma**, a 36-year-old mother of three, whose eyes had dulled over time like metal forgotten in the rain. Her husband had died four years ago. Since then, she had withdrawn. She no longer laughed. She no longer cooked with joy. Her children often found her sitting alone, staring into nothing.

She had seen Mama Khosi many times for headaches and chest tightness. She had taken the tea for "soul fatigue." She had prayed. But something remained.

Today, for the first time, the healer and the therapist would speak with her together.

Mama Khosi:

Noma, my child, we have walked many times together. You have trusted me with your dreams, your sicknesses, your quietness. Today, I want you to meet someone who listens in another way. She listens to the heart like I listen to the bones.

Nora (smiling gently):

Thank you, Mama. Noma, I've heard from others that your body often feels tired, even when you've rested. That sometimes you feel far away, even when you're here. Is that true?

Noma (quietly):

Yes. I am here but I do not feel inside myself anymore. I feel... hollow. Even when people talk to me, it feels like they are speaking through water.

Mama Khosi (nodding):

You have carried much grief, and grief has no clock. I have seen this before—when sorrow sits too long, it begins to change the body. But there is also a wound here. (She gently places her hand over her chest.) *Not a sickness, but a silence.*

Nora:

When you think about your husband's passing, what do you feel inside?

Noma:

Nothing. Then pain. Then shame because I am still angry at him for leaving me. But I never say it out loud. Who would understand that I blame a dead man?

Mama Khosi (softly):

You see? That is a story hidden in the body. It is not the spirits who make her heavy. It is the words that never left her mouth.

Nora:

May I tell you something, Noma? In the kind of work I do, we believe that stories—especially the painful ones—get trapped when they are not told. They begin to live in the body. Your headache, your tight chest, the tiredness... these may be your spirit's way of asking you to speak.

Noma (voice trembling):

I do not even know what I feel anymore.

Mama Khosi:

Then let us help you remember. I will give you herbs to help your sleep. Nora will sit with you and help you find your words. This is not about choosing between the old ways and the new. This is about using all the ways to bring you home to yourself.

Over the next few weeks, Noma visits the compound regularly. After each session with Nora, she sits with Mama Khosi for tea. The healer blesses her before she begins to speak. The therapist listens, never rushing, never pushing.

Slowly, Noma begins to unravel the knot in her chest. She speaks of her husband's sudden illness. Her fear of not being enough. Her guilt for wanting joy again. Her anger at God. Her secret hope that maybe—just maybe—she is still allowed to live.

She cries.

She breathes.

She begins to laugh, hesitantly at first, as if remembering how.

And when villagers ask if she's better, Mama Khosi replies:

"She is healing from the inside out. The herbs opened her sleep. The words opened her soul."

Two Healers, One Vision

In villages like Mbali, the bridge between traditional healing and therapy does not need to be wide. It only needs to be walked by two people willing to share the load of a suffering soul.

Mama Khosi continues her work, but now she understands that some wounds are buried beneath herbs and prayer.

Nora continues her sessions, but she knows the land, the drum, and the ancestors also speak to healing.

Together, they have learned that **depression is not just sadness—it is silence**, and **therapy is not just science—it is listening**, and **healing is not just one tradition—it is whatever brings the person back to life.**

In the stillness of early morning, when the sun has not yet touched the rooftops and the roosters are clearing their throats, there is a sound in the village that many cannot hear.

It is not the rhythm of the drum.

Not the rustle of maize in the wind.

It is the sound of what is **not said**—passed from one generation to the next like a woven basket that carries both harvest and hardship.

In these quiet villages, where culture is rooted deep and families are built wide, children grow up surrounded by stories—but often, **not the ones that matter most.**

They know who to greet and when.

They know how to fetch water, kneel in respect, and carry firewood with balance.

They know which relative fought in the war and which ones are not to be mentioned.

But what they rarely know is *why their mother does not laugh anymore,*

why their father drinks alone,

or *why they themselves feel scared even when nothing has happened.*

When Silence Becomes a Spirit

In the hills of eMpangeni, where the sun rises slowly over the sugarcane fields and the evenings hum with quiet prayers, there is a story that repeats itself with different names and faces, but always with the same heartache.

It begins with silence.

Not the gentle silence of peace, but the heavy silence of inheritance—the kind that is passed from grandmother to mother, from father to son, like a whisper too afraid to become words.

This silence does not make noise, but it speaks loudly in the way people carry themselves:

- In the hunched shoulders of women who have buried too much pain.
- In the clenched jaws of men who were never taught how to cry.
- In the tired laughter at funerals.
- In the way no one asks, *"Are you really okay?"* because everyone assumes suffering is just part of life.

And when this silence grows unbearable, it does not always lead people to therapy—it leads them to the *thwasa* path, the road of traditional healing.

There are many who say they are being called to become sangomas. They dream of snakes, hear drumming in their sleep, or feel an unshakable illness that no clinic can diagnose.

And yes—some are truly called.

Some are chosen by the ancestors, gifted with sacred sight, and destined to heal others through traditional means.

But others... others are not being called.

They are crying.

They are mothers whose unresolved grief has turned into nightmares.

They are young women who have been silenced after trauma.

They are men who were never taught how to express heartbreak.

They are people looking for meaning when pain has no name.

And when no one in the community talks about depression, when no one suggests therapy, when emotional pain is still seen as weakness or witchcraft, these people interpret their suffering as a spiritual calling.

"I keep getting sick—I must be ignoring the ancestors."

"Maybe I need to become a healer so I can finally find peace."

But what they truly need is someone to ask:

"What broke your heart?"

Unacknowledged pain never disappears.

It settles in the chest.

It tightens in the stomach.

It climbs into the head as headaches that no medicine can cure.

In time, it becomes high blood pressure, chronic fatigue, even stroke.

In one village, a man named Sipho became known as "the one who refused the calling." He resisted the dreams, refused to train as a healer, and instead drank until the dreams turned to static. At fifty-two, he collapsed while feeding his goats—his third stroke in four years. But no one ever asked what he was grieving.

In another homestead, MaZanele went through *ukuthwasa* (initiation) after years of illness. She was finally "cleansed," but her heart still ached. She later confided to a traveling nurse:

"I thought becoming a sangoma would fix my pain, but I realize now, I never mourned my firstborn child. I buried him and I buried myself too."

What might have happened if Sipho had been seen by a therapist instead of dismissed as stubborn?

What if MaZanele had been offered grief counseling after her loss, before the community insisted it was a calling?

Therapy is not the enemy of tradition. It is the **missing mirror** that could help people distinguish between a spiritual call and emotional collapse.

In the absence of therapy, becoming a healer becomes the only legitimate language for deep emotional disturbance.

It becomes refuge.

It becomes reason.

It becomes the only explanation for why someone cannot breathe at night.

There are traditional healers who understand this difference—who know when a person is not called, but simply carrying too much pain.

They refer such individuals quietly, gently, to nurses, to counselors, to social workers.

But the majority still operate in a space where emotion is spiritualized, and so depression is not treated, only named something else.

Without integration between mental health services and traditional structures, the silence continues, and people continue to fall—quietly, invisibly—into chronic illness, into brokenness, into avoidable death.

What if every traditional healer had access to basic psychoeducation?

What if every clinic in the village had a room for talking, not just for tablets?

What if people were taught that sometimes, the dream is not a calling—it is trauma trying to speak?

What if we could say, with love and without shame:

"You are not cursed. You are grieving. You are not being called. You are collapsing."

And what if we made room for both healing traditions—those of the ancestors, and those of the inner self?

In the end, not every illness is ancestral.

Not every silence is sacred.

Not every burden needs to become a career in healing.

Sometimes, all that is needed is for the pain to be named.

Sometimes, therapy is not the enemy—it is the interpreter of pain that never got to speak.

Until the day therapy becomes part of the village's language of healing, many will continue to mistake the ache in their chest for a calling.

But perhaps, one story at a time, we can help them see:

You are not being summoned to heal others yet. You are being invited to finally heal yourself.

Children in rural communities are keen observers. They see everything—the way their parents' eyes avoid each other at dusk, the shift in breath when certain names are mentioned, the sudden tension that enters a room without explanation.

But without anyone to explain emotions, without the space to ask questions, they begin to internalize what they don't understand.

They may think:

- *"Maybe Mama is sad because of me."*
- *"Maybe men are supposed to be angry all the time."*

"Maybe silence is the price for peace."

When Children Inherit What Was Never Theirs

In Mogalakwena District, in the heart of Mokopane, where the land is wide and the mountains hold secrets older than maps, children play with sticks and stones in the dust. Their laughter fills the air like birdsong, and their feet are toughened by earth and running.

But listen closely—not to what they say, but to what they carry.

Before these children can spell their names, before they can trace the shape of an "A" or the curl of an "M," they are already bearing burdens that were never theirs to carry.

They inherit them like heirlooms:

- A mother's quiet rage folded neatly into the way they flinch at sudden noise.
- A father's unspoken shame stitched into their silence when asked how they feel.
- A grandmother's heartbreak passed down not in words, but in warning: *"Be strong."*

These children, even before they can speak full sentences, are already living inside the pain of their families—pain that has no name, no ceremony, and no rest.

The Language Before Language

In a small preschool outside of Mahwelereng, a teacher noticed something strange: a boy who never cried. Even when he fell and bled, he would stand up, wipe the dirt from his knees, and look away.

When asked why, he said, *"Crying is for babies. My uncle said so."*

He was four years old.

Another little girl refused to play in groups. She said the laughter of others made her nervous. No one had hit her. No one had shouted. But her mother, just nineteen herself, had grown up in a house of yelling, and now, without knowing it, lived in fear and passed it on like breath.

These are not isolated cases. They are echoes of unresolved pain, traveling through generations like dust that settles in new rooms.

Psychoanalysis—a form of deep emotional and psychological exploration—tells us that trauma does not need to be spoken to exist. It lives in gestures, in avoidance, in repetition.

In Mogalakwena, it lives in the way children sit stiffly at mealtime.

In the way boys tease each other to hide tenderness.

In the way girls become mothers to their siblings before their own voices are fully formed.

13. What Is Psychoanalysis, and Why Here?

Psychoanalysis is often misunderstood. People think of couches in big cities, of distant European theories and complicated terms. But in truth, psychoanalysis is the art of listening to what was never said.

It asks:

- What did you not get to say as a child?
- What pain are you repeating, hoping to finally resolve it?
- Whose suffering are you carrying inside your chest?

For children in Mokopane, where therapy is rare and emotional language is limited, psychoanalysis offers a quiet room, a safe adult, and permission to feel.

It says: *"Let us find the beginning of your pain—even if you don't have words for it yet."*

And often, it is in silence that children begin to speak—not with mouths, but with drawings, behavior, and patterns.

In one family near Ga-Madiba, three generations lived under one roof.

The grandmother, strong and stoic, had lost her husband to minework and never remarried.

Her daughter, now forty, was withdrawn, spending most days cleaning or praying, her laughter a memory.

The granddaughter, only ten, had begun skipping school, complaining of stomach aches that doctors could not explain.

The school referred her for counseling.

In the sessions, it was revealed that the girl was terrified of being "left behind." Her father had disappeared years ago. She had no language for abandonment, but she felt it in her body.

Psychoanalytic intervention showed that her pain was not just hers—it was part of a chain of unresolved grief, passed down, unspoken.

The therapist worked not just with the child, but with the mother and grandmother—helping them give words to what had been kept in silence for decades.

Tears came.

Then stories.

Then, for the first time, peace.

In villages like Mokopane, therapy is still viewed with suspicion. People ask:

- *"Why do you need to talk to a stranger?"*
- *"Are you mad?"*
- *"Don't you have family to talk to?"*

But what happens when the family is the source of silence?

What happens when no one knows how to hold pain, only how to bury it?

This is why psychoanalysis is so important—not because it replaces tradition, but because it **restores the voice of the inner child**. The one who was told to stop crying. The one who was left behind. The one who still lives in every adult who feels broken and doesn't know why.

THE HEALING WE NEVER SPOKE OF: THERAPY

Imagine a different Mogalakwena.

One where every school had an emotional wellness facilitator.

Where a child could say, *"I don't know why I'm sad,"* and be met with understanding, not dismissal.

Where parents were taught that silence is not always strength.

Psychoanalysis offers that dream—not in the form of textbooks, but in the form of patient, compassionate exploration. It asks each person:

What did you have to forget to survive?

Can we remember together, safely?

In Mogalakwena, before a child learns to speak, they already live inside a story. But they deserve to write their own.

Psychoanalysis is not the only tool, but it is a powerful one. It teaches us that the past is never just the past. It lives in the present, until it is understood, spoken, and released.

And so, in the dusty villages where children still chase chickens and dodge cows in the road, let us give them more than schoolbooks.

Let us give them the freedom to feel.

The permission to speak.

The healing they didn't know they needed.

Because a village that listens to its children is a village that has begun to heal itself.

Without psychoanalytic therapy—or any emotional processing support—they often grow up misreading their feelings as personal flaws rather than signals of buried family pain.

A child who acts out in school might be seen as disrespectful.

A teenager who avoids company may be labeled shy.

A young girl who starts crying at night with no reason is often told to "be strong."

But underneath these behaviors are **emotional legacies**:

- A father who never spoke of the beatings he endured as a boy.
- A mother who was silenced when she cried as a child.
- A household that never said "I'm sorry," only "move on."

And so the children don't learn language for their inner world. They learn to survive it.

They become adults who say, *"I'm fine,"* when they are not.

They raise their own children with quietness and discipline, not realizing they are repeating the very pattern that hurt them.

In urban settings, a struggling child might eventually be sent to a counselor or therapist. But in rural villages, the idea of a child needing **emotional support**—let alone psychoanalysis—is often unheard of.

"What could a child be stressed about?"

"They have food and clothes. What more do they want?"

"They must be bewitched."

These are not cruel words—they are inherited misunderstandings.

They reflect a world where pain is physical, not emotional, and where strength means not speaking.

But children do feel.

They do carry.

And they do break, silently, without a sound.

Without intervention or healing space, this silence grows roots. And over the years, it becomes:

- Boys who think they must prove their worth through anger.
- Girls who learn that quietness is love.
- Young people who leave the village not just for jobs—but for freedom from a house that never heard their truth.

And when they become parents, they often repeat the only model they knew: *Don't speak. Don't cry. Don't ask.*

And so, the chain continues.

Imagine, for a moment, a village where therapy is not feared but embraced. Where storytelling becomes part of school. Where children are asked, *"How does that make you feel?"* as often as *"Have you done your homework?"*

Imagine elders trained to listen not just with their ears, but with emotional awareness.

Imagine a boy sitting with a community counselor, saying:

"When my father yells, I feel like I disappear."

And the counselor replies:

"You matter. Let's find the part of you that is still standing."

This is not a dream. It is a possibility—if psycho-emotional care is woven into the fabric of village life, not as a foreign concept, but as an extension of traditional wisdom.

Because even traditional culture once had its own form of therapy—in storytelling, in songs of sorrow, in fire-side confessions. It only needs to be remembered.

Children in the villages do not need to inherit silence.

They need to be given permission to feel.

To ask.

To grieve.

To be told, *"You are not weak because you are hurting."*

Without therapy, their pain finds other places to live—on their skin, in their fists, or in their silence.

But with care, with space, and with the language of healing, they can finally say what generations before them never could:

"This pain stops with me."

14. Where Herbs and Emotions Can Meet

This is not an argument against herbs. Quite the opposite. The wisdom of traditional healing is profound and sacred. Plants have power. Nature offers real medicine. But what if herbs could be accompanied by emotional inquiry? What if healers could also become listeners—not just to the body, but to the stories behind the pain?

In a quiet village on the dusty outskirts of Mokopane, where the fig trees grow thick and the air smells of burnt offerings and ancestral smoke, there lived a man known by many names—*Ntate Thembani, Ngaka ya Moya, Baba wa Lesedi*. People came to him with problems both physical and unseen: strange dreams, aching bones, troubled marriages, lost fortunes.

He would grind herbs in a mortar older than the village clinic. He would throw bones across a woven mat and listen with his whole body. His hut was filled with bottles, feathers, and smoke that curled like ancient whispers.

He was trusted. Respected. Feared.

But at night, Thembani could not sleep.

He would sit up, drenched in sweat, his chest tight with something he could not name. He had dreams that felt more like memories, and memories that refused to become dreams. Sometimes, the drumming in his ears was not from the ancestors—but from the pounding of anxiety that refused to leave.

He had not told anyone. How could he? He was the healer. The conduit. The chosen.

To admit his pain would mean... what, exactly? Weakness? Disrespect to the calling?

So he continued. Helping others. Cleansing others. Guiding others.

Until the day he met Dr. Naledi Seboko, a psychoanalyst visiting the district to work with children who had survived domestic violence. They met at a local community workshop organized by a women's support group. She was speaking about trauma—the kind you don't always remember but feel every day.

Her words felt like medicine, not in the body, but in the soul. And when she spoke of **emotional inheritance**, something in Thembani's chest stirred.

Later that evening, under the old fig tree where he often meditated, Thembani invited Dr. Seboko to sit.

The sun was dying softly behind the mountain, and the birds had stopped singing.

Thembani: "You speak of pain passed from mother to child. Do you believe that... spirits carry these things?"

Naledi (smiling gently): "Not in the way you mean. But yes, I believe the soul carries what the mouth never spoke. Sometimes for generations."

Thembani: "Then perhaps I am not a healer. Perhaps I am just a man who never cried enough."

Naledi said nothing. Silence, to her, was often more useful than any response.

Thembani: "There was a time I believed I was chosen. I was sick for many years. Strange dreams. Then the elders confirmed it—I had the calling. I went through *ukuthwasa*. And I did feel better. For a time."

Naledi: "But?"

Thembani: "But I never dealt with the reason I became sick. The things I saw as a boy. What my father did to my mother. What my uncle did to me when I was twelve. I never told anyone. Instead, I became a healer. Now... I see their pain in everyone I treat. But I cannot touch my own."

Naledi placed her hand gently on the mat between them. A soft invitation.

Naledi: "Ntate Thembani, this is not a dismissal of your gift. The work you do is sacred. But sacred work can also wound the worker. Psychoanalysis is not a replacement. It is a return—to the moment where you stopped feeling safe, and where the story changed."

He looked down at his hands. Strong hands. Hands that had buried elders and birthed hope.

Thembani: "But if I go back... I might not come back whole."

Naledi: "Then let someone walk with you. Even the strongest tree bends in the wind. Even the healer must sit at someone else's fire, sometimes."

When the Bones Cannot Speak

Over the next weeks, Thembani allowed himself to talk. Not publicly. Quietly. Privately. With Naledi.

She never asked about the ancestors. She asked about childhood, about shame, about the first time he felt invisible. And he realized something:

There had never been a space where he was just a boy.

He had gone from being a survivor to being a vessel.

From brokenness to holiness—with no time to heal in between.

He did not stop his traditional work. In fact, his visions became clearer. His energy stronger. His sleep—less haunted.

He began telling some of his patients:

"This pain needs both herbs and honesty."

"Speak to someone trained in feelings—not just spirits."

And because they trusted him, they listened.

This is not a story against herbs.

Nor is it a war between healing traditions.

This is a call to remember that even those chosen to carry the pain of others must **lay down their own sorrow** somewhere. That traditional healing is sacred, but so too is sitting down and saying: *"This happened to me, and it hurt."*

In the villages of Mogalakwena and far beyond, the wisest healers are now beginning to walk beside therapists, not behind them or against them. They speak of ancestors—and of abuse. They burn imphepho—and refer for counseling. They understand that true healing is not either/or, but *everything together*, in its rightful time.

And sometimes, the most powerful healing begins not with a bone reading or a diagnosis, but with a single question whispered beneath a tree:

"Have you told your own story, Ngaka?"

THE HEALING WE NEVER SPOKE OF: THERAPY

Imagine an elder who not only gives a herbal drink for sleep but gently asks,

"What is troubling your heart these days?"

Or a community health worker who says,

"This pain might be from your body—but it may also be your spirit asking to be heard."

In this way, healing becomes complete.

There is a growing need to build a bridge between traditional healing and mental health awareness. Rural communities do not need to choose between herbs and therapy—they can have both. But first, they must be helped to see that the two are connected.

That headache is not just about poor sleep.

That fatigue is not just about a long day.

That heaviness in the chest is not always a sickness of the body.

Sometimes, it is grief with no name.

Anger with no outlet.

Fear with no language.

When people begin to understand that depression and stress can cause real physical symptoms, they begin to reframe their pain. They begin to look inward, not just outward. They begin to ask not only "What will cure this?" but "What caused this?"

That is where healing begins.

Rural communities are not without intelligence. They are not without strength. But they are often without space—space to feel, to speak, to explore the unseen.

When we help women and men in these areas to see that the body and emotions are not enemies, but companions...

When we honor their herbs while also honoring their heartbreak...

When we teach that depression is not a failure, but a signal...

Then, and only then, will true healing take root.

Let the herbs remain. Let the land continue to offer its gifts.

But let us also offer something new: the permission to feel, the wisdom to explore emotion, and the courage to believe that healing can come not only through leaves—but through listening, through love, and through the language of the heart.

Through techniques like narrative therapy, bodywork, mindfulness, talking circles, or simply quiet conversation, therapy becomes a space of returning—to voice, to worth, to self.

When a woman begins to believe her emotions matter, something powerful happens. She no longer serves from emptiness. She no longer teaches her daughters that silence is the price of love. She no longer accepts pain as destiny.

Her healing becomes generational.

Other women begin to notice. They ask, "Why do you look lighter these days?" She might say quietly, "I started talking to someone." And the seed is planted.

In this way, therapy is not just about feelings. It is about freedom. It is about rewriting the story that suffering is all there is. It is about giving women back what culture tried to steal—the right to feel, to speak, to be whole.

To every woman who has told herself she doesn't matter: you do.

To every woman who has stayed silent because that's what she was taught: your voice matters.

To every woman who believes emotional pain is just her fate: healing is possible.

Therapy is not a place of weakness. It is a place of return. A return to the truth that you are not a machine. You are not a servant. You are not a sacrifice.

You are a human being. And your feelings are not in the way—they are the way home.

Emotional isolation becomes a form of self-preservation, a shield against a world that may not listen or understand.

Yet this isolation is not without cost. Suppressed emotions often manifest as physical illness, depression, anxiety, or a deep sense of emptiness. The woman who "seems fine" on the outside may be carrying decades of pain with no words to describe it.

In many rural cultures, honor is deeply tied to a woman's behavior. Women are often seen as carriers of family honor, and any perceived weakness or disobedience can be seen as dishonor.

Admitting emotional distress may be interpreted as bringing shame to the family, leading to further restrictions or social exclusion.

Because of this, even when therapy is available, women may avoid it altogether—fearing that opening up will bring more harm than healing.

In many rural communities, there is a quiet truth that few dare to speak out loud: people are hurting, deeply, but silently. You see it in the tired eyes of a mother who cannot sleep at night, in the short temper of a father who drinks to forget, in the withdrawn silence of a young girl who once sang to the sky but now barely speaks.

But when you ask, "How are you?" the answer comes quickly—too quickly.

"I'm fine."

"We're managing."

"There's no need to talk about it."

This silence is not because people feel no pain. It is because they carry something heavier than pain—shame.

Shame, in village life, is a wall. It is thick and invisible, yet it blocks the road to care. It whispers, *"If others find out, they will laugh."* It warns, *"A real man does not cry."* It reminds women, *"Good wives do not complain."* So people smile through sorrow and pretend that all is well, even when they are breaking inside.

At the same time, there is **honor**, a deeply rooted value in village communities. Honor can be beautiful—it teaches respect, dignity, and pride in one's family. But when misunderstood, honor becomes a **chain**—a chain that silences suffering. Many believe that to admit emotional pain is to bring shame upon the family name. A man with anxiety hides it. A woman with depression prays harder but tells no one. A teenager with suicidal thoughts is told to be strong and keep quiet.

And so, the wall stands tall. The chain grows tighter. And suffering continues—in silence, behind closed doors.

But what if there was a way out? What if there was a place where pain could be spoken without judgment, where fear could meet compassion, and where shame had no voice?

That place exists. It is called therapy.

In a therapy session, no one laughs when you say you are tired of pretending. No one mocks you for crying. Instead, you are listened to. Carefully. Gently. A therapist does not come to judge. They come to understand. They come to walk with you through the hard places of your heart, and help you make sense of what has felt too heavy for too long.

For rural communities, therapy might sound unfamiliar or foreign. Some think it is only for "crazy" people or those who are weak. But that is a lie. Therapy is not weakness. It is wisdom. It is strength to say, "I cannot carry this alone." It is courage to say, "I want to live fully, not just survive."

In villages where gossip spreads fast and privacy is rare, therapy offers a safe and sacred space—sometimes with someone from outside the village, so that the talking can be truly free. There are even group therapy models where people support one another in healing, slowly learning that they are not alone.

With therapy, shame begins to crack. Honor takes a new shape—not as silence, but as bravery. A man who seeks help becomes an example for his sons. A woman who speaks her truth helps her daughters do the same. Families begin to heal, not by hiding their pain, but by facing it together.

We must begin to teach our rural communities that it is not dishonor to feel, that there is no shame in healing. Pain is not a weakness—it is part of being human. And no wall or chain should keep a person from the help they need.

The truth is simple: therapy works. It can save marriages. It can restore broken hearts. It can prevent suicide. It can make space for joy again.

And the more we talk about it, the more we bring therapy out of the shadows and into the community. Not as a strange thing, but as a gift—one that belongs to everyone, whether they live in cities or under the wide sky of the village.

Let us help one another climb the wall of shame. Let us break the chain of silence. Because healing begins the moment we are brave enough to speak—and wise enough to listen.

The silence of rural women is not a sign of weakness—it is a reflection of a system that has failed to hear them. To break these walls, we must begin by listening with compassion, not judgment. Community-based therapy models must be culturally sensitive, rooted in trust, and delivered in ways that respect local traditions while gently challenging harmful norms.

Creating safe, private spaces—even small ones—can be powerful. Trained women facilitators, community health workers, or peer mentors can provide entry points into healing. Group storytelling, art therapy, and mother's circles can become tools to gently unlock buried emotion.

Education also plays a key role. Teaching emotional literacy in schools, training local leaders on mental health awareness, and involving religious or cultural leaders in the conversation can slowly shift mindsets. When emotional wellbeing is normalized and valued, women will feel safer to speak.

Behind every silent woman in the village is a story of strength—of surviving, adapting, and carrying on despite unspoken pain. But strength should not require silence. As therapists, advocates, and community members, we must work to create a world where rural women no longer feel they must hide their hearts to survive.

Let their voices be heard. Let healing begin not with loud declarations, but with quiet courage—and with someone who finally asks, "How do you feel?" and truly listens.

15. Why Village Men Avoid Seeking Help

In the context of rural life, masculinity is often defined by strength, stoicism, and silent endurance. For men living in villages, this traditional understanding of what it means to "be a man" often leaves little space for vulnerability, emotional expression, or the seeking of support. Especially when it comes to marital difficulties, many men choose to suffer in silence rather than admit they are struggling. The reluctance to seek professional help is not a sign of indifference or lack of emotion—but rather, it is the outcome of deep-rooted cultural expectations, social pressures, and internalized shame.

In most traditional village settings, a man's identity is closely tied to his ability to **provide, protect, and lead**. He is expected to control his household, maintain discipline, and act as the final decision-maker. When problems arise in his marriage—be it emotional distance, communication breakdowns, or conflict—seeking help from a therapist or outsider may feel like an admission that he has failed in his most basic role.

For many men, this loss of control can be deeply humiliating. The idea of sitting down with a therapist to "talk about feelings" may seem incompatible with how they've been taught to respond to challenges. Instead of opening up, they may withdraw, resort to anger, or try to fix the problem silently, all while burying their own pain.

The fear of being judged—by family, peers, and the community—is a powerful deterrent. In village life, privacy is scarce. A man seeking help for "marriage problems" might be seen as weak, incapable, or even as someone whose wife has gained power over him—an image that directly contradicts traditional masculine pride.

This shame is not only external; it is also internalized. Many men have never been taught the language of emotional expression. They may not even recognize that what they are feeling is stress, sadness, or helplessness. Instead, they experience emotional distress through physical symptoms (such as headaches, insomnia, or fatigue) or behavioral changes (such as drinking, avoidance, or aggression), all without acknowledging the root cause.

In many rural cultures, the family is seen as a private unit, and problems are expected to be resolved "within the home." Seeking therapy or external support may be viewed as exposing family issues to outsiders—a betrayal of trust, or an act of disloyalty to one's wife or parents.

Men, especially those raised in conservative households, may feel obligated to protect the family's reputation above all else. Rather than share their struggles with a professional, they may turn to friends, religious leaders, or no one at all. The belief that "real men handle their own problems" continues to act as a barrier to therapeutic intervention.

Many men in rural villages have had little opportunity to explore or understand their own emotional lives. Raised with the idea that crying is for women or that talking about feelings is a weakness, they often grow up emotionally disconnected—from themselves and others. This emotional illiteracy makes therapy intimidating, even alien.

Therapists who attempt to engage men in rural settings must first understand this reality. The goal is not to force emotional disclosure but to **build trust slowly**, often by framing therapy not in emotional terms, but in practical ones: problem-solving, improving family life, or reducing stress.

To encourage more men to seek help, especially during marital struggles, mental health services must adapt in language, approach, and accessibility. Some effective strategies include:

The Role of Community Models and Celebrities in Changing the Narrative

In rural areas where tradition holds deep influence, social norms are often slow to change. Mental health, in particular, remains a taboo subject—surrounded by shame, fear, and misunderstanding. Yet change is possible, and it often begins with a single voice. When respected individuals—especially male leaders, elders, or celebrities—speak openly about mental health, they do more than just share their stories. They redefine strength, challenge stigma, and inspire others to follow a new path toward healing.

This chapter explores how community role models and public figures can open doors that therapy alone cannot—and how their leadership may hold the key to reshaping attitudes in even the most conservative rural settings.

In villages, trust is not easily given. Outsiders, including therapists, health workers, or aid agencies, may be welcomed cautiously—but not always embraced. However, respected men within the community—village elders, school teachers, religious leaders, former chiefs, or successful farmers—hold a special status. Their words carry weight. Their example sets the tone for others.

When these men talk about seeking help—whether for emotional exhaustion, relationship problems, or personal trauma—they send a powerful message: you are not weak for speaking up. In fact, you are brave. You are wise. You are protecting yourself and your family.

Such openness, especially when shared in local languages and in culturally appropriate ways, helps normalize vulnerability. It creates space for others to say, "If he can talk about it, maybe I can too."

For example, an elder respected for his wisdom might share that after the death of his son, he spoke to a community counselor and found peace. A young teacher might admit that stress from family expectations pushed him to the edge, but therapy helped him recover. These small truths can ripple across the village and change hearts in ways that public campaigns alone cannot.

Celebrity Influence and the Reach of Media

In addition to local role models, celebrities and public figures—especially those from rural or humble origins—have enormous potential to shift mental health narratives. When a well-known athlete, musician, or actor speaks out about emotional challenges or therapy, the effect can be transformative.

Young people in rural areas often look up to celebrities, even more so with increasing access to radios, mobile phones, and television. A short radio interview where a singer talks about growing up poor and struggling with depression, or a documentary where a football star discusses the pressure of expectations and seeking counseling, can be deeply impactful.

These public figures offer relatable success stories, not because they are perfect, but because they are honest.

In every village, there are those who rise—through music, sports, storytelling, or public service—and become local legends. These individuals, often born into the same humble conditions as their neighbors, carry a special kind of influence. They are known. They are respected. And most importantly, they are believed.

When such figures—rural-born celebrities—share their own experiences with therapy and emotional healing, they can disarm stigma, inspire confidence, and make mental health support feel reachable for the everyday person. In communities where therapy is still misunderstood or feared, a familiar voice from someone who "made it" can serve as a bridge between tradition and modern healing.

At the heart of this approach is authenticity. Village celebrities who have gone through their own personal struggles—be it with grief, stress, burnout, addiction, or marital conflict—can make a deep impact by speaking honestly about those challenges.

A folk singer might tell a crowd how she nearly gave up performing after the death of a sibling, and how speaking to a counselor helped her regain her voice. A footballer raised in a farming village might talk about the pressure to succeed and how therapy helped him manage anxiety. A storyteller or poet may reflect on childhood trauma and how healing was found not only in words but in guided emotional support.

When these stories are told in the local dialect, rooted in the rhythm of the people's everyday lives, they become more than stories—they become mirrors. They let villagers see their own pain and possibilities reflected through someone they admire.

Here are key ways rural celebrities can integrate their personal therapy stories into community mental health work:

Organizing tours where the celebrity visits different villages to share their story, speak openly about therapy, and answer questions. These events could be hosted in schools, churches, cultural halls, or marketplaces. A short performance or talk followed by a candid conversation can reduce fear and promote curiosity.

Radio remains one of the most trusted and accessible forms of communication in rural areas. Celebrities can appear on talk shows or storytelling segments to discuss emotional struggles in a natural, unscripted way. By using humor, warmth, and humility, they help make therapy a normal part of life conversations.

Artists can weave themes of emotional struggle and healing into their work—songs about loss and recovery, poems about pain and resilience, short plays that depict the courage of seeking help. These works can travel far and be shared in schools or community events.

Celebrities can help organize community wellness days where they appear alongside local therapists, health workers, or counselors. Their presence can reduce fear and draw crowds. A person might come to hear their favorite singer—but leave with a referral to a mental health professional.

Imagine a small therapy room or mobile counseling unit named after a beloved village hero—"The Healing Room of Mama Lela" or "Coach Okello's Peace Corner." By lending their name, celebrities help remove shame and offer a familiar presence in the healing process.

It is crucial that the message of healing be delivered in culturally respectful ways. Celebrities must avoid the impression that therapy is a "Western idea" forced onto rural communities. Instead, they can speak about therapy using familiar values:

- "Talking to someone wise" instead of "counseling."
- "Unburdening the heart" instead of "mental illness."
- "Strengthening the mind" instead of "psychological help."

When therapy is framed as a modern extension of traditional wisdom, more people feel safe enough to listen.

Not everyone will accept the message at first. Some may mock it. Others may deny they need help. But when the celebrity stays consistent, shares without shame, and refuses to glorify suffering, a cultural shift begins. The people start to ask questions. Young men begin to wonder if they too can be strong and still feel. Mothers begin to think about their daughters' mental health. Teachers start to listen to children differently.

The celebrity, once a symbol of fame, becomes a symbol of healing.

The most powerful thing a rural celebrity can say is not, "I am perfect," but, "I was hurting too—and I found help." In doing so, they become a new kind of hero—not one who hides pain behind a smile, but one who shows that courage lives in vulnerability, and that strength includes the willingness to heal.

Therapy is no longer something foreign. It becomes a part of the story, a stepping stone in a life that others can aspire to.

Let the heroes of the villages rise—not just to entertain or inspire, but to heal and lead their people toward a future where no one has to suffer in silence again.

Their fame allows them to break the silence in a way that feels safe, even admirable. When they tell rural men, "It's okay to get help," they offer permission that society otherwise denies.

Importantly, celebrity engagement must be authentic. Token endorsements or scripted campaigns may be dismissed. But when a celebrity shares a genuine, heartfelt story—especially if they have walked a similar path as rural men—the connection is real.

Stigma thrives in silence. It tells men to hide their pain, to mask their emotions, to cope alone. But when community leaders and celebrities share their stories, they do something radical: they break the silence. They say, "You are not alone." This creates a domino effect—one person's honesty inspires another, and another, until a new culture of acceptance begins to grow.

We must also remember that stigma is not only personal; it is structural. When a chief or mayor supports local mental health services, or when a famous singer donates to a community wellness center, they send a message that therapy is not just acceptable—it is a public good, a source of strength, something worth investing in.

By lending their voice, time, and platform, role models help reframe mental health from a problem of weakness to a matter of collective strength and dignity.

To harness the power of role models, communities must create intentional platforms where these voices can be heard. This includes:

- Community gatherings or open forums where respected elders speak about emotional resilience.

In every society, people look to leaders for permission—permission to speak, to act, to feel. When respected men and well-known public figures lead by example, they give others the courage to follow.

In rural communities, where silence has too long been mistaken for strength, the voices of role models are needed now more than ever. They have the power to tell a different story—one where men are not alone in their suffering, where seeking help is seen as responsibility, not weakness, and where emotional health is part of what it means to be truly human.

Let them speak. Let them be heard. Because in their honesty lies the beginning of a better, more compassionate future.

The silence of men in rural communities is not because they lack emotion—it is because they have been taught to hide it. The marital struggles they face, and the internal conflicts they endure, are real and often painful. By understanding the roots of their reluctance and by offering culturally respectful, community-based approaches, we can create safe spaces where men feel permitted to speak—not just as husbands or providers, but as human beings.

True strength is not the absence of vulnerability—but the courage to face it.

16. Overview of Therapy in the Villages and Rural Set up

Providing therapy services in villages and rural areas is crucial for addressing the unique challenges faced by these communities, such as social isolation, limited healthcare access, and stigma associated with mental health issues. These communities also have distinct cultural norms and values, which therapists working in these areas can better understand and address. Additionally, offering therapy services in villages can reduce barriers to access, as many individuals may face transportation or financial difficulties.

Research has shown that some individuals, particularly Black women, may have reservations or challenges in seeking therapy for depression due to cultural and familial attitudes, perceived ineffectiveness of therapy, and the Strong Black Woman (SBW) role.[2] These factors can lead to a reluctance to seek professional help, questioning the value and impact of therapy on mental health. Additionally, some participants may only consider seeking therapy when their symptoms become severe or when all other informal sources of support are exhausted. Despite these challenges, a significant portion of participants endorsed seeking therapy as a form of self-care and resistance against societal norms, recognizing the importance of prioritizing mental health and challenging traditional cultural norms.[2]

The study reveals various reasons for depression help-seeking behavior, emphasizing stigma, positive mental health treatment images, and culturally sensitive services to support individuals hesitant to seek therapy.

South Africa's political landscape has significantly affected rural health care practice and access to services.

Over half of the country's population lives in rural areas, with a significant percentage of poor individuals. Rural South Africans face health challenges like poverty and chronic disabilities. High transportation costs, long distances, and traditional beliefs hinder access to healthcare. Rural hospitals and clinics provide limited diagnostic services. Mental health care in rural South Africa is limited and fragmented, with a lack of resources and professionals. Community-based approaches, collaboration between healthcare providers and informal healers, cultural relevance, and alternative interventions are recommended to address these challenges.[3]

The Chinese attitude towards therapists and mental health services is changing, but it varies between individuals and regions. Historically, there has been a stigma associated with mental health problems in China, which has led to a lack of use of mental health services. Many Chinese have not sought treatment or treatment for psychiatric disorders, and many people have not been treated. This hesitation to seek help has been influenced by cultural factors, lack of awareness and historical low priority mental health in China: Challenges and progress.[4]

The study in Jimma Zone, Oromia, Ethiopia, revealed that many residents have inadequate knowledge about mental health issues, including misconceptions about psychiatric disorders and living alone as a treatment. However, some symptoms of mental illness were recognized. The findings underscore the need for public education and mental health literacy programs. However, there was recognition of certain symptoms of mental illness, such as talking or laughing alone and displaying unusual behaviors.[5]

The research effectively combines emotional, empirical, and systemic arguments to establish the significance of the issue of marriage denial for gay men and lesbians.[6] The article highlights the injustice and inequality of marriage denial for gay men and lesbians, highlighting the fundamental institution of marriage in American culture. Unlike heterosexual citizens, they are denied benefits, restricting their citizenship and harming their mental well-being. The article explores the impact of marriage denial on their mental health and analyses historical and cultural factors.

The historical context of how homosexuality was viewed in the U.S., including as a sin, disease, and crime, is discussed to provide insight into the stereotypes and discrimination faced by gay men and lesbians. (6) It highlights the historical stereotypes and discrimination faced by these individuals, which have no scientific basis and are used to justify denying them the right to marry or be parents. The article also highlights the shift in societal attitudes towards same-sex relationships, but also highlights the negative stereotypes and opposition to legal recognition of same-sex partnerships. The denial of marriage rights is seen as reinforcing the stigma associated with sexual identity, particularly affecting adolescents and young adults who seek to openly express their sexuality.[6] In conclusion, the article argues for recognizing the right to choose one's partner as a fundamental aspect of sexual citizenship, emphasizing that this right continues to be denied to gay and lesbian citizens in the United States.

Rural therapy faces unique ethical dilemmas and decision-making challenges, particularly in implementing urban ethical standards. Rural practitioners often struggle to apply these codes effectively due to real-life ethical dilemmas.[7] They also face multiple relationships with clients and community members, which create ethical complexities. Issues like competence, limited resources, geographic isolation, community values, and inter-agency working relationships contribute to these challenges. Rural practitioners often rely on a combination of internalized ethical stances and formal codes.[7]

Understanding these dilemmas is crucial not only for rural practitioners but also for their urban colleagues, policymakers, and professional organizations.[7] Ethical practice in rural settings requires a thoughtful and evolving approach that considers the unique dynamics and challenges of these communities. Open discussions and ongoing examination of ethical standards are essential to ensure the well-being of clients and practitioners in rural therapy settings.

Traditional, complementary, and alternative medicine (TCAM) is a range of healthcare practices outside the conventional system, particularly in Sub-Saharan Africa (SSA).[8] It includes indigenous remedies like herbal medicines and imported therapies like acupuncture and chiropractic care. TCAM has a significant economic impact, contributing at least R2.9 billion (US$2.2 million) to the South African economy. However, challenges remain, such as lack of comprehensive policies, insufficient research infrastructure, and limited regulation. Recognizing TCAM's importance is crucial for effective healthcare policies and practices in the region. TCAM has a long history in SSA, with a substantial portion of the population relying on these practices to address various health concerns, both communicable and non-communicable. [8]

Tesfaye and colleagues, 2021 reveals that mental health problems are influenced by biological, psychological, and cultural factors, with brain dysfunction, excessive worry, accidents, and family conflicts being the most common causes which is consistent with findings from Nigeria, northern Ethiopia, and Denmark.[5] Factors like sex, residence, and education level influence mental health knowledge. Most respondents recognize mental illness manifestations, and over three-quarters believe recovered patients can be productively employed. Treatment combines medical, religious, and traditional approaches. Respondents with basic reading and writing skills were 64% less likely to have adequate knowledge compared to those with at least a secondary school education.[5]

However, other studies in Tanzania, Eritrea, and Saudi Arabia pointed to biological factors as the primary causes. Societal factors influence mental illness causes, with diverse explanations based on socioeconomic, literacy, and urban-rural differences. Treatment combines medical, religious, and traditional methods, as seen in Eritrea, Saudi Arabia, Nigeria, and Ethiopia.[5] However, other studies in various countries had differing findings, indicating the diversity of treatment perspectives across different regions.

There are several critical problems in mental health services in villages, with a focus on the context of Namibia. According to Coomer 2013, several systemic challenges in accessing and receiving quality mental healthcare services in rural Namibia. [9] Poor service provision, lack of expertise, language barriers, transportation challenges, financial barriers, and prioritizing education are the main issues faced by participants. Nurses are often perceived as rude or unhelpful, and there is a lack of continuity in healthcare specialists. [9] Patients also face difficulties in accessing doctors due to their unavailability and the stressful nature of hospital visits. Financial barriers, such as hospital consultation fees and government disability grants, are also reported.[9] Access to education is a higher priority than healthcare services, and poverty significantly impacts mental health. Public awareness and information dissemination are also crucial. Disability grants are also challenging to access due to lengthy registration processes and associated costs.[9]

Hansen et al, 2021 reveals that parents face significant barriers when seeking help for their child's mental health issues. (10) Symptom duration and severity are key factors, with severe cases encountering the highest barriers. Lack of knowledge about where to seek help is another barrier, with delays in recognizing mental health problems contributing to this. Stigmatization and parent blame are also significant barriers. The multi-agency nature of child mental health services also poses challenges, with unavailability of services, professionals refusing to initiate interventions, and lack of communication between services.[10] The study recommends targeted training for professionals and increased public and professional knowledge about mental health services.

A study comparing patient interactions with Western healthcare providers and traditional healers in sub-Saharan Africa found that patients preferred traditional healers due to their patient-centered communication and alignment with their understanding of illness.[11] The study involved 43 patients receiving care from Western healthcare providers and 35 from traditional healers, with 40 patients providing informed consent and 35 agreeing to participate in the study. This contrasts with Western consultations, where providers typically interrogate patients about symptoms. The study suggests that integrating patient-centered communication into public health services could enhance perceived quality of care and healthcare program effectiveness. However, limitations include a small sample size of traditional healers, socio-demographic data, and unclear communication differences. Further research is needed to validate these findings and explore the effectiveness of promoting a patient-centered approach among Western healthcare providers.

This study aimed to understand the pathways to mental health care in Africa by analyzing 14 studies from four African countries (Ethiopia, Nigeria, South Africa, and Zimbabwe). [12] The study found that traditional and religious healers are often the first to provide mental health care, especially in Nigeria. Delays in accessing formal services are linked to consulting these healers.

Factors like stigma, service availability, cost, and patient satisfaction influence help-seeking behaviors.[12]

The escalating rate of divorce among black South Africans has raised concerns about the future of marriage within African society, which traditionally values the sanctity of marriage. [13] Indigenous African marital therapy, as outlined by Sodi et al. and others, aims to address marital conflicts and reconcile couples rather than promoting divorce. Indigenous African marital therapy emphasizes communal aspects of marriage, with elders acting as jurors and conflict resolution. It values parental guidance and respects elders' wisdom. Despite urbanization and changing societal norms, preserving traditional values can strengthen and enduring marriages among black South Africans.

Pastoral therapy, a spiritual approach, has limitations in addressing marital issues in black African communities due to its disregard for indigenous African traditions and values. [13] To address these shortcomings, proponents argue for integrating indigenous African marital therapy with pastoral counseling to create a more comprehensive and culturally relevant approach. Divorce, a complex process in African societies, is influenced by factors like age, childlessness, laziness, infidelity, communication issues, financial hardships, falling out of love, and lack of commitment.[13] Missionaries who introduced Christianity and pastoral counseling in Africa often disregarded indigenous African traditions and values, favoring

Eurocentric approaches. [13] The main problems for men in therapy, revolve around the weight of societal stigma associated with mental illness, particularly in the context of masculinity and gender norms. [14] Men with mental health issues often face internalized stigma, leading to feelings of fear, shame, embarrassment, guilt, and isolation. Mental illness stigma is a complex issue influenced by negative attitudes from peers, family, healthcare professionals, and the community, often leading to fear and shame among young men. This stigma is exacerbated in male-dominated environments, leading to concealment of mental health struggles. [14] It also intersects with other forms of social marginalization, such as sexual orientation, race, and class.

The study highlights China's mental health challenges, including uneven development of services across regions, low continuing professional development (CPD) among mental health professionals, and low ethical regulations in mental health organizations. [15] The study suggests that socioeconomic development plays a crucial role in the availability and quality of mental health care. It also underscores the need for comprehensive regulations and policies to guide mental health professionals and improve service quality.

Other approaches in therapy

The review of Traditional, Complementary, and Alternative Medicine (TCAM) use in Africa highlights the need for incorporating TCAM modalities into healthcare training institutions and promoting continuous education. [16] High utilization is driven by perceived low cost, alignment with sociocultural values, and dissatisfaction with conventional healthcare. TCAM is often used alongside conventional medicine, but potential herb-drug interactions need clinical studies. Socioeconomic factors influence TCAM use, with low-income individuals more likely.[16] Existing studies have methodological limitations and require improved research quality and standardization.

Challenges in the isolated semi urban areas

Mental health for farmers is crucial for their overall quality of life. [17] Factors such as long hours, unpredictable weather, financial strain, work-life balance, limited access to mental health services, and dealing with uncertainties like weather patterns and market conditions can affect their mental well-being. Support systems like family, friends, and community networks can help reduce feelings of isolation and provide a safety net during challenging times. Self-care practices, such as taking breaks and engaging in leisure activities, can also help farmers. Increasing awareness about mental health issues and reducing stigma is essential for farmers to seek help when needed. [17] Government agencies and communities can provide resources and initiatives to support farmers' mental health. [17] Holistic approaches, such as mindfulness practices, yoga, and nature-based therapy, can also help reduce stress and improve mental health.

In many villages and rural areas, access to mental health services and trained therapists can be limited, which can pose challenges for individuals seeking therapy. [18]

Traditional healing practices and community-based support systems may play a significant role in addressing mental health concerns in such areas, as they are often more accessible and culturally relevant. However, it is crucial to note that traditional therapies may not always provide the same level of evidence-based treatment as modern psychological therapies. The effectiveness of therapy, whether traditional or modern, also depends on the nature and severity of the mental health condition. [18] Some conditions may respond well to traditional practices, while others may require specialized psychological interventions or medication. In summary, the effectiveness of therapy in villages and rural areas can vary, and the choice between traditional and modern therapy should be made based on the individual's needs, the availability of services, and cultural considerations.

Access to mental health services and trained professionals remains a significant challenge in many rural areas, highlighting the need for improved mental health care infrastructure in these regions.[18]

The overarching theme highlighted the significant influence of husbands in family planning decision-making, often resulting in women feeling the need to seek their husbands' consent before taking any family planning action. [19] The study involved postpartum women, their partners, health workers, and village health team members (VHTs) in Uganda. Initially, 26 postpartum women were identified for individual interviews, with 22 eventually participating.[19]Of these, 12 partners were also interviewed, and three couples were interviewed during the antenatal period. A total of 34 focus groups were conducted, involving 323 participants, with an average of nine participants per group. The study found that couples often lack awareness of each other's views on family planning, highlighting the need for improved communication and counseling. Barriers to counseling include time, location, cultural stigma, and HIV testing inclusion.[19]

The role of how therapy can assist patients

The crisis of mental health in China is characterized by a significant gap between the growing demand for mental health services and the limited resources available to address this demand.[20] Rapid urbanization and economic growth have led to new mental health challenges in the country. Historically, mental health services have been low, leaving 173 million people with psychiatric disorders untreated. The Chinese government has improved services, but challenges remain, including migrant workers' mental health needs and high suicide rates. The crisis highlights the urgent need for accessible, dependable, and affordable mental health care in China. [20]

The study explores the relationship between cultural norms, masculine expectations, and mental health among African men.[21] It reveals that societal expectations, particularly in African culture, can lead to risky behaviors like risky sexual behavior, alcohol use, and reckless driving. Masculine norms, characterized by restrictive emotionality, also impact men's mental health, leading to increased stress, denial of emotional symptoms, and unhealthy coping mechanisms like substance abuse.[21] The study suggests targeted interventions and policies to address these issues, emphasizing the importance of awareness, psychological referral, and person-focused therapy.

Eloped women face societal challenges and stigmatization due to gender roles and patriarchal norms. [22] They are often seen as a betrayal of family ties and virtue, while men are less stigmatized and can return to their families easily. Eloped women also experience social exclusion and judgment within their communities, leading to a lack of participation in rituals and ceremonies. Financial insecurity is another significant challenge, as they often start their married lives independently without traditional support.[22] Inheritance rights are also a concern, and women may face psychological trauma and torture-related risks. In extreme cases, their families to preserve honour may trap them into prostitution or face murder attempts.

The study conducted in Nigeria focused on understanding the factors influencing the initiation of treatment for individuals with schizophrenia.[23] It found that the duration of untreated psychosis, which can have long-term effects on the outcome of the disorder, is influenced by various factors. Traditional and faith healers often result in significant delays before patients seek help from psychiatrists. Additionally, family influence, particularly in developing countries, plays a significant role in the choice of the first treatment provider. The study revealed that despite limited mental health resources in Nigeria, a substantial proportion of individuals initially seek help from prayer houses, which are considered places of spiritual healing.

Treatment failure for mental disorders in villages is often due to patients' belief in curedness, lack of social support, mobility, stigma, poor communication, disintegrated hospital systems, and traditional treatment. [24] Factors such as belief in curedness, lack of social support, mobility, denial of mental disorder severity, poor communication, and challenges with staff, medicines, side effects, and unclear communication contribute to treatment default.[24] To improve treatment outcomes, it is crucial to address these socially-derived factors, implement tailored health education, and explore collaboration between traditional and medical practitioners. Further research should investigate demographic variables associated with treatment default in these settings.

The study conducted in the Eastern Cape with participants aged 45 to 60 revealed several key themes related to the status of mental health in the region.[25] The first theme highlighted the negative impact of mental illness within family structures, leading to strained relationships and increased financial burden as families provide support and care for affected individuals. The second theme underscored the desperation of indigenous people to access a cure for mental illness, often resorting to traditional healers in addition to Western methods.

The third theme indicated insufficient knowledge about mental illness, with families feeling confused and emotionally affected due to a lack of awareness campaigns. Lastly, the fourth theme explored various perceptions and beliefs among indigenous people regarding the origins of mental illness, including witchcraft, jealousy, amafufunyana, ukuthwasa, and ancestral anger. (25) These findings highlight the complex socio-cultural factors influencing mental health in the Eastern Cape and underscore the need for targeted awareness campaigns, improved access to mental health services, and collaboration between Western and traditional healing practices to address the challenges faced by affected individuals and their families.

The research discusses how rural values, such as self-reliance, conservatism, lack of trust in outsiders, strong work ethic, and an emphasis on family and individualism, impact the utilization of mental health services in rural areas negatively.[26] It highlights that general medical doctors often provide mental health assistance in rural communities due to biases and a lack of desire to refer patients to mental health professionals.

Additionally, the research emphasizes the stigma surrounding mental health in rural communities, the lack of anonymity for those seeking mental health services, and the challenges of implementing physical healthcare in such areas. Counselors in rural communities face unique ethical and boundary issues, often necessitating a wider range of care. To address these issues, the research suggests strategies such as education to reduce stigma, understanding the nature of the counseling process, and networking for consultation and support.[26]

The study discusses rural mental health disparities in the United States and emphasizes the use of the National Institute on Minority Health and Health Disparities (NIMHD) research framework to understand and address these disparities. [27] The NIMHD framework considers multiple dimensions and levels of influence on mental health outcomes, offering a comprehensive approach. Rural residents face unique challenges, including limited access to specialty mental health care, geographic isolation, stigma, and socioeconomic factors.

The study provides a hypothetical example of an individual in a rural community to illustrate the complexities of accessing mental health care in such areas.

The research highlights the urgent need to address mental health disparities among rural populations, particularly in children, adolescents, older adults, and racial/ethnic minorities.[27] Suicide rates are significantly higher in rural areas, and suicide prevention efforts need to be culturally appropriate and specific to rural communities. The study calls for innovative research designs, including those that test interventions to reduce stigma, improve access to care, and promote engagement with mental health services. Overall, it underscores the importance of considering multiple domains and levels of influence when studying and addressing mental health disparities in rural settings.

The examination of Paul Bohannon's Six Stations of Divorce and Reva Wiseman's emotional and psychological stages provides a comprehensive understanding of the divorce process. Both models shed light on the intricate and multifaceted nature of divorce, with Bohannon focusing on external stages and Wiseman on internal emotional experiences.[13] This analysis underscores the complexity of divorce, especially within African societies where marriage is deeply significant. It highlights various contributing factors and triggers for divorce while emphasizing the importance of addressing multiple dimensions of healing, including spiritual, social, physical, psychological, and environmental aspects. Furthermore, the study underscores the relevance of indigenous African marital therapy as a valuable resource in guiding individuals and couples through the challenges of divorce, ultimately promoting stronger marriages and families within African communities.

The diverse perspectives and knowledge regarding the causes and treatments of mental health problems among respondents. It underscores the importance of considering factors such as education, gender, and residence when addressing mental health awareness and education programs.[5] The findings of recent studies and community-based observations suggest that mental illness is not experienced or understood in a uniform way across all societies. Rather, it emerges as a complex and deeply layered phenomenon, shaped by the interplay of biological, psychological, and cultural dimensions. This understanding challenges the notion of a one-size-fits-all model for diagnosis or treatment, highlighting the importance of context in both the experience and expression of mental distress.

From a biological perspective, mental illness is often linked to imbalances in brain chemistry, genetics, or other neurological and physiological processes. Conditions such as depression, anxiety, or schizophrenia may have identifiable biological markers or familial patterns that help to explain their origin. However, while biology can provide part of the answer, it does not encompass the full human experience of suffering. In many societies, particularly in rural or indigenous communities, this biomedical explanation may feel distant or disconnected from the lived reality of people's lives.

The psychological dimension addresses the individual's internal world—how thoughts, emotions, and behavior interact. Factors like unresolved trauma, prolonged stress, grief, and learned coping mechanisms all contribute to psychological distress. Psychoanalytic thinkers such as Sigmund Freud and Carl Jung have long emphasized that inner conflict, unconscious repression, and early childhood experiences profoundly shape mental health. In the context of traditional societies, however, these psychological narratives may be interpreted through symbolic language, dreams, ancestral messages, or spiritual imbalances—highlighting a different but equally valid understanding of emotional pain.

Most significantly, cultural interpretations of mental illness vary dramatically across regions and communities such as Limpopo Province. In some rural areas, symptoms of depression may not be verbalized as sadness or hopelessness, but rather experienced as physical ailments—chronic headaches, fatigue, stomach problems, or spiritual disturbances. People may not speak of "anxiety," but describe it as "a tight chest" or "a weight in the stomach." In certain traditions, hearing voices may not be immediately pathologized, but seen as a call to spiritual duty or a connection to ancestral guidance.

These culturally rooted understandings are not merely semantic differences—they shape how people seek help, who they trust, and whether they believe healing is possible. In some villages, a traditional healer may be consulted long before a psychologist is ever considered. In others, a pastor, elder, or community leader may provide spiritual comfort and interpretation for what in Western settings would be considered a psychiatric condition.

Since he comes from the province of Limpopo, Branny Mthelebofu has observed and recognised that in cultures where emotional language is encased in spiritual or collective symbolism, it is important to adapt treatment methodologies to include narrative, metaphor, ritual, music, and prayer. In this lifetime, prayer is important for resolving issues that require therapy, and therapy may also help them by employing a prayer method. The majority of people in the province of Limpopo are spiritual and think that culture may help them work out problems with one another.

The book also reveals a generally optimistic outlook regarding the recovery and productivity of individuals with mental health issues, which could be a positive sign for reducing stigma and promoting inclusion. Overall, this research underscores the importance of addressing mental health from a holistic perspective, taking into account the multifaceted nature of the condition and tailoring interventions to the specific needs and beliefs of different communities.

In conclusion, progress in addressing men's mental illness stigma necessitates researchers to explore and expand the broader stigma and mental health literature, focusing on the intersections of masculinities and stigma, to inform the development of effective, relevant, and appealing destigmatization interventions.[28]

Rural therapy can fail for patients due to a combination of limited access to specialized mental health services, a shortage of trained professionals, and unique ethical challenges in small-community settings.

In the heart of Limpopo Province, where mountain shadows dance across maize fields and herders sing softly to their goats, healing is not a solo act. It has never been. Long before clinics, long before terms like "trauma" or "psychological repression" were spoken, the people here knew that healing begins with gathering.

Beneath trees.

Around fires.

In rondavels and church halls.

In whispers between women washing clothes by the river.

In conversations between uncles and sons walking back from the fields.

But something happened along the way.

Modern pain—silent, private, invisible—slipped through the cracks of these traditional gatherings. People began to suffer inwardly, hiding sorrow beneath work, worship, or weary smiles. Women bore the burden of obedience. Men carried the silence of duty. Children learned too early to keep secrets.

And now, in places like **Mogalakwena, Ga-Mashashane, and Botlokwa**, new wounds meet old customs.

What, then, does healing look like for this generation?

It begins, not in a clinic, but in a circle.

Imagine this: a community center in a dusty Limpopo village. Inside, a circle of chairs has been placed with intention. No one is in front. No one is behind. There is no stage, no pulpit. Only a **circle**, like the sun, like the moon, like the drums of their ancestors.

In this circle are women and men, elders and young adults, teachers, farmworkers, sangomas, nurses, pastors—and a trained psychoanalyst, not here to lecture, but to listen.

This is not group therapy as imagined in textbooks.

This is circle psychoanalysis—culturally adapted, locally grounded, spiritually aware.

It is healing in a language the people already speak.

The facilitator, a young clinical psychologist from Polokwane, begins not with diagnostic language, but with a question:

"What stories did you inherit that you never agreed to carry?"

At first, there is silence. The kind of silence that has lived too long in many throats.

Then a woman in her fifties, wrapped in a faded headscarf, speaks.

"My mother told me that a good woman never raises her voice. Even when she's hurting."

There is a murmur in the circle. Not judgment. Recognition.

A man follows.

"I was told to be strong. That crying makes you less of a man. But my son died last year. And I haven't cried yet."

The psychologist doesn't offer solutions. Not yet. She allows the silence after the words to stretch long enough for truth to settle.

This is how it begins. Each story, like a stone dropped in a still dam, sends ripples.

The circle taps into what psychoanalysis calls the "unconscious shared experience." In African settings, this concept is embodied through Ubuntu—*I am because we are*. Healing is not a private task. It is a communal return to emotional dignity.

In these group sessions:

17. Psychoanalysis Beneath the Baobab Tree

The village did not need fixing.

It needed listening.

And listening—deep, careful, respectful listening—was always at the heart of what Sigmund Freud first imagined when he spoke of psychoanalysis. Long before therapy rooms with cushioned chairs and hour-long sessions behind closed doors, Freud's earliest vision was of talking. Talking that heals. Talking that reveals. Talking that frees the soul from what it does not know it carries.

In rural Limpopo, talking had always been there. Around fires. At water taps. In the slow turn of stories told by grandmothers. But for years, no one thought to look there for therapy.

Until now.

When the psychoanalyst arrived in the village of **Ga-Mashashane**, she came not with white coats or notepads, but with a chair in a circle and ears tuned not to pathology, but to people.

She had studied Freud in Johannesburg—*the unconscious, defense mechanisms, repression*. But in the village, she began to understand something else:

That Freud's work was never meant to stay in Vienna.

It was meant to travel to wherever people hide parts of themselves to survive.

Speaking the Unspoken in Sepedi and Song

The circle of chairs was made beneath a large **marula tree**. Some women came with babies tied to their backs. Some men came with folded arms and skeptical eyes. The healer sat nearby too—not as a competitor, but as a companion in the room of the spirit.

The psychoanalyst began not with theory, but with a proverb.

"Motho ke motho ka batho."

(A person is a person through others.)

And slowly, stories began to unfold.

A woman spoke of a miscarriage never mourned.

A boy spoke of beatings he never questioned.

An old man wept for the first time since burying his son during the pandemic.

They spoke in **Xitsonga, Tshivenda, Setswana, Sepedi**. No translation was needed. Grief does not require subtitles.

Freud had once said:

"Where id was, there ego shall be."

But here, it became:

Where silence was, there truth shall speak.

One woman, named **Khutso**, shared a dream. She had it every month: she was standing at a riverbank with no bridge. Her late grandmother stood on the other side, calling her by name, but she could never cross.

In classical psychoanalysis, dreams are the royal road to the unconscious. And in the village, dreams are also messages from the ancestors.

So instead of interpreting the dream away, the psychoanalyst asked:

"What stops you from crossing the water?"

Khutso whispered, "I carry too much."

And in that moment, something shifted. The circle saw it too. The dream was not about death. It was about burden. About unspoken grief. About guilt and duty and being the strong one for too long.

Freud would have called it repression—feelings too dangerous to feel, tucked away deep in the unconscious, leaking out through dreams, illness, tension.

But here, they just called it *"what we've never said out loud."*

No Diagnoses, Only Invitations

The psychoanalyst never labeled anyone.

She did not say, *"You have PTSD."*

She said, *"When did the crying stop? And who told you to stop it?"*

She did not say, *"You are emotionally avoidant."*

She said, *"When you were a child, who listened when you were afraid?"*

Hierarchy dissolved.

An elder woman's tale of losing five children to illness in the 1970s was held with the same care as a young man's silent nod after admitting he had thought of ending his life.

There was no stage.

No authority.

Only a guest with questions.

Freud in the Village: An Unexpected Home

Could Freud have imagined this?

A psychoanalytic process not in a clinic but in a circle beneath a marula tree, between the language of the unconscious and the language of the ancestors?

Perhaps not. But if he had been there, he might have recognized it anyway:

THE HEALING WE NEVER SPOKE OF: THERAPY

The return of the repressed, when a man cries for the first time in thirty years.

The working through, as a woman links her anger at her husband to her father's silence.

The free association, when people begin to speak without being asked.

The transference, when the group becomes a surrogate family.

The healing, not from analysis alone—but from being witnessed, safely and fully.

In Limpopo, healing must wear many garments.

It can come as prayer.

As herbs.

As rhythm.

As memory.

But it can also come in talking circles, guided gently by psychoanalytic insight—not to replace tradition, but to reveal what tradition sometimes silences.

The goal is not to dissect the villagers.

The goal is to restore them to themselves.

And Freud, in his deepest wish, wanted just that: to help people uncover what they had hidden, to live not from fear, but from freedom.

So yes—psychoanalysis can live here.

It just has to remove its shoes before entering the circle.

"Where do you feel this pain in your body?"

"Whose voice is it that told you to hide your sadness?"

"What do you want to say that you've never said aloud?"

Week by week, as people return to the circle, something shifts.

A woman who never cried begins to weep freely.

A man who sat with folded arms now leans in.

A sangoma and a nurse begin to speak of grief in the same breath—one through dreams, one through memory.

The group begins to understand something profound:

That emotional wounds passed down from generation to generation can be named—and then released.

One man shares:

"I became a sangoma after many deaths in my family. But I now realize I was also carrying depression. My ancestors were calling, yes. But I was also trying to heal something in myself that no one saw."

There is no shame in this sharing. Only relief. Only recognition.

Ripples in the Village

Soon, those in the circle begin to influence those outside of it. A woman tells her daughter it's okay to cry. A man speaks to his teenage son about heartbreak.

The circle becomes more than a support group. It becomes a soft revolution.

Church leaders begin to ask for workshops on emotional intelligence. Sangomas begin referring clients who carry "unseen wounds" to mental health professionals. Village councils discuss allocating space for community mental health gatherings.

In Limpopo, where culture runs deep and change walks slowly, this is not a rejection of tradition—it is a revival of it.

The healing circle is not a foreign concept. It is simply the return of voice to the places where silence was once a virtue.

Psychoanalysis, when braided with tradition and adapted to the soil of Limpopo, does not erase culture. It honors it. It adds the missing language for pain that had no words. It provides the space for people to say:

"This is what happened to me. And I want to understand why I still carry it."

And perhaps, most powerfully, it allows them to realize:

They are not alone. They never were.

Would you like the next chapter to focus on how to train community members as paraprofessional facilitators to sustain these circles after the psychologists leave?

The scarcity of resources and mental health professionals in rural areas may result in delayed or inadequate treatment, leaving patients without timely support. Additionally, ethical dilemmas arising from overlapping relationships and the integration of personal and professional roles can compromise the quality of care, potentially leading to negative outcomes for patients.

Based on the findings and insights presented in the book, here are some recommendations for addressing the challenges and improving mental health care and therapy services, particularly in rural and culturally diverse settings:

Mental health education and awareness programs are essential for promoting understanding and addressing mental health issues. Mental health professionals should be trained to be culturally competent and sensitive to diverse beliefs and practices. Community-based approaches can help reduce stigma and promote mental health awareness. Traditional healing practices can be incorporated with evidence-based psychological therapies. Anti-stigma campaigns can challenge negative attitudes and promote open discussions. Access to services should be improved, especially in rural and underserved areas. Early intervention and prevention strategies should be focused on. Support for caregivers and families should be provided. Interdisciplinary collaboration among healthcare providers is encouraged. Policy and funding support should prioritize mental health funding, especially in rural areas. Specialized mental health programs should be developed for specific populations. Regular training and continuing education are essential. These recommendations aim to create a more inclusive, culturally sensitive, and accessible mental health care system that addresses the unique challenges faced by individuals and communities in various geographic and cultural contexts. Implementing these recommendations requires collaboration among healthcare providers, policymakers, community leaders, and mental health advocates to ensure that mental health care becomes more equitable and effective for all.

18. Declaration

I declare that there is no conflict of inters in this book.

19. References

1. Khan, T. A., Hamid, W., & Swalehin, M. (2022). Social Exclusion and the Runaway Couples: A Study of Their Hardships. Contemporary Voice of Dalit, 14(1), 8–24. https://doi.org/10.1177/2455328X211000566
2. Nelson, T., Shahid, N. N., & Cardemil, E. V. (2020). Do I Really Need to Go and See Somebody? Black Women's Perceptions of Help-Seeking for Depression. Journal of Black Psychology, 46(4), 263–286. https://doi.org/10.1177/0095798420931644
3. Vergunst R. From global-to-local: rural mental health in South Africa. Glob Health Action. 2018;11(1):1413916. doi: 10.1080/16549716.2017.1413916. PMID: 29320947; PMCID: PMC7012042.
4. Shi W, Shen Z, Wang S, Hall BJ. Barriers to Professional Mental Health Help-Seeking Among Chinese Adults: A Systematic Review. Front Psychiatry. 2020 May 20;11:442. doi: 10.3389/fpsyt.2020.00442. PMID: 32508688; PMCID: PMC7251144.
5. Tesfaye, Y., Agenagnew, L., Anand, S. et al. Knowledge of the community regarding mental health problems: a cross-sectional study. BMC Psychol 9, 106 (2021). https://doi.org/10.1186/s40359-021-00607-5
6. Herdt, G., Kertzner, R. I do, but i can't: The impact of marriage denial on the mental health and sexual citizenship of lesbians and gay men in the United States. Sex Res Soc Policy 3, 33–49 (2006). https://doi.org/10.1525/srsp.2006.3.1.33

7. Schank, J. A. (2009). Ethical Issues in Rural Counselling Practice. Canadian Journal of Counselling and Psychotherapy, 32(4). Retrieved from https://cjc-rcc.ucalgary.ca/article/view/59087
8. James PB, Wardle J, Steel A, et al. Traditional, complementary and alternative medicine use in SubSaharan Africa: a systematic review. BMJ Glob Health 2018;3:e000895. doi:10.1136
9. Coomer RA. The experiences of parents of children with mental disability regarding access to mental health care. Afr J Psychiatry (Johannesbg). 2013 Jul;16(4):271-6. doi: 10.4314/ajpsy.v16i4.36. PMID: 24051566.
10. Hansen AS, Telléus GK, Mohr-Jensen C, Lauritsen MB. Parent-perceived barriers to accessing services for their child's mental health problems. Child Adolesc Psychiatry Ment Health. 2021 Jan 29;15(1):4. doi: 10.1186/s13034-021-00357-7. PMID: 33514400; PMCID: PMC7847149.
11. Labhardt ND, Aboa SM, Manga E, Bensing JM, Langewitz W. Bridging the gap: how traditional healers interact with their patients. A comparative study in Cameroon. Trop Med Int Health. 2010 Sep;15(9):1099-108. doi: 10.1111/j.1365-3156.2010.02575.x. Epub 2010 Jun 9. PMID: 20545920.
12. Burns JK, Tomita A. Traditional and religious healers in the pathway to care for people with mental disorders in Africa: a systematic review and meta-analysis. Soc Psychiatry Psychiatr Epidemiol. 2015 Jun;50(6):867-77. doi: 10.1007/s00127-014-0989-7. Epub 2014 Dec 12. PMID: 25515608; PMCID: PMC4442066.
13. TLHARIHANI, Baloyi and OLEHILE, Buffel. The phenomenon of divorce and its challenge to the black

African communities: A need for pastoral and indigenous African marital therapy. STJ [online]. 2021, vol.7, n.2 [cited 2023-09-24], pp.1-21.

14. McKenzie SK, Oliffe JL, Black A, Collings S. Men's Experiences of Mental Illness Stigma Across the Lifespan: A Scoping Review. Am J Mens Health. 2022 Jan-Feb;16(1):15579883221074789. doi: 10.1177/15579883221074789. PMID: 35125015; PMCID: PMC8832600.
15. Qian M, Chen R, Chen H, et al. Counselling and psychotherapy services in more developed and developing regions in China: A comparative investigation of practitioners and current service delivery. International Journal of Social Psychiatry. 2012;58(5):536-543. doi:10.1177/0020764011413669
16. James PB, Wardle J, Steel A, et al. Traditional, complementary and alternative medicine use in SubSaharan Africa: a systematic review. BMJ Glob Health 2018;3:e000895. doi:10.1136/ bmjgh-2018-000895
17. Deegan, D., Fingleton, E., McEvoy, J.J. and Quigley, K. (2023), "Nurturing mental health and well-being using ordinary farms", Irish Journal of Occupational Therapy, Vol. 51 No. 1, pp. 1-5. https://doi.org/10.1108/IJOT-07-2022-0026
18. James PB, Wardle J, Steel A, et al. Traditional, complementary and alternative medicine use in SubSaharan Africa: a systematic review. BMJ Glob Health 2018;3:e000895. doi:10.1136/ bmjgh-2018-000895
19. Willcox ML, Mubangizi V, Natukunda S, Owokuhaisa J, Nahabwe H, Nakaggwa F, et al. (2021) Couples' decision-making on post-partum family planning and antenatal counselling in Uganda: A qualitative study. PLoS ONE

16(5): e0251190. https://doi.org/10.1371/journal.pone.0251190[1]

20. Xiang YT, Yu X, Sartorius N, Ungvari GS, Chiu HF. Mental health in China: challenges and progress. Lancet. 2012 Nov 17;380(9855):1715-6. doi: 10.1016/S0140-6736(11)60893-3. PMID: 23158236.
21. Ezeugwu CR, Ojedokun O. Masculine norms and mental health of African men: what can psychology do? Heliyon. 2020 Dec 10;6(12):e05650. doi: 10.1016/j.heliyon.2020.e05650. PMID: 33336092; PMCID: PMC7734219.
22. Khan, T. A., Hamid, W., & Swalehin, M. (2022). Social Exclusion and the Runaway Couples: A Study of Their Hardships. *Contemporary Voice of Dalit, 14*(1), 8–24. https://doi.org/10.1177/2455328X211000566
23. Odinka, Paul C., et al. "The Socio-demographic Characteristics and Patterns of Help-Seeking among Patients with Schizophrenia in South-east Nigeria." Journal of Health Care for the Poor and Underserved, vol. 25 no. 1, 2014, p. 180-191. Project MUSE, https://doi.org/10.1353/hpu.2014.0055.
24. Mokwena, K.E.; Ndlovu, J.Why Do Patients with Mental Disorders Default Treatment? A Qualitative Enquiry in Rural Kwazulu-Natal, South Africa. Healthcare 2021, 9, 461. https:// doi.org/10.3390/healthcare9040461
25. Booysen, D., Mahe-Poyo, P., & Grant, R. (2021). The experiences and perceptions of mental health service provision at a primary health centre in the Eastern Cape. *South African Journal of Psychiatry, 27*, 8 pages. doi:**https://doi.org/10.4102/sajpsychiatry.v27i0.1641**
26. Carter, Danessa, "Providing counseling in a rural setting: a

1. https://doi.org/10.1371/journal.%20pone.0251190

new multicultural perspective" (2019). Graduate Research Theses & Dissertations. 4574. https://huskiecommons.lib.niu.edu/allgraduate-thesesdissertations/4574

27. Morales DA, Barksdale CL, and Beckel-Mitchener AC. (2020) A call to action to address rural mental health disparities. Journal of Clinical and Translational Science 4: 463–467. doi: 10.1017/cts.2020.42
28. McKenzie SK, Oliffe JL, Black A, Collings S. Men's Experiences of Mental Illness Stigma Across the Lifespan: A Scoping Review. Am J Mens Health. 2022 Jan-Feb;16(1):15579883221074789. doi: 10.1177/15579883221074789. PMID: 35125015; PMCID: PMC8832600.

Did you love *The Healing We Never Spoke Of: Therapy*? Then you should read *My Wedding Contract Too*[2] by Branny Smith and Branny Smith!

[3]

When a woman discovers a shocking mistake in her husband's death and marriage certificates, she is drawn into a legal battle for ownership of the family business and her late husband's estate, pitting her against her best friend.

2. https://books2read.com/u/md9xo5

3. https://books2read.com/u/md9xo5

About the Author

Branny Mthelebofu is a multifaceted South African creative whose work bridges the realms of storytelling, healing, and music. As a filmmaker, nutrition therapist, holistic counsellor, and musician, he channels his diverse talents into narratives that explore the complexities of the human psyche and the pursuit of inner peace.

Under the pen name Branny Smith, Mthelebofu crafts stories that delve into personal challenges, emotional trauma, and the transformative journey toward self-understanding. His literary works, such as The Professor's Descent, Desperation, and Chasing Where There is Love, My Wedding Contract Too, Her Lover is Gone, often feature protagonists grappling with internal conflicts and societal pressures, reflecting his deep interest in mental health and psychoanalysis. Beyond writing, Smith employs his background in holistic therapy to assist clients in achieving emotional well-being through interactive counselling sessions. His approach integrates scriptwriting principles to facilitate character development and personal growth, offering a unique therapeutic experience that resonates with individuals seeking happiness and fulfillment.

As a musician, Branny Smith composes lyrics that address life's challenges, happiness, and the quest for peace of mind, utilizing music as a form of therapy for his audience. His passion for mental health and storytelling converges in his creative endeavors, making his work a compelling exploration of the human condition.

Through his multifaceted career, Branny Smith Mthelebofu continues to inspire and guide others on their journeys toward self-discovery and emotional resilience.

Read more at https://brannysmith.hearnow.com/so-my-lover.

Banny Joma

All about
Research

About the Publisher

The publisher produces films, sound tracks, music (different genres) and also publishes books.

www.ingramcontent.com/pod-product-compliance
Lightning Source LLC
LaVergne TN
LVHW090405210926
848480LV00002B/457